# CHRISTIAN MARRIAGE

Paul E Brown

**GRACE PUBLICATIONS TRUST**
7 Arlington Way
London EC1R 1XA
England

e-mail: editors@gracepublications.co.uk
www.gracepublications.co.uk

Managing Editors:
M. J. Adams and D. Crisp

© Grace Publications Trust
First published 2014

ISBN: 978–1–910137–05–5

Distributed by
EP BOOKS
Faverdale North Industrial Estate
Darlington DL3 0PH
England
e-mail: sales@epbooks.org
www.epbooks.org

Printed by Bell and Bain Ltd, Glasgow

# Acknowledgements

I am very grateful for the editorial assistance of Don Crisp. I also owe a great debt to my wife, Mary. We have gone through the book together more than once, considering both contents and expression. Our marriage of more than fifty years has greatly helped in the writing of this book.

# Contents

# Introduction

Throughout the history of the human race marriage has generally been the basic building block of society. Marriage between a man and a woman forms the beginning of a family. As children are born they are brought up in the love and security that comes from two people committed to each other and to each new arrival. When the children grow up, they too can form families of their own. The whole human race has developed in this way.

This book has been written because of the need for Christians to develop a biblical understanding of marriage. Even Christian couples have too often been married with little idea of what marriage entails or what the Bible teaches. Sometimes there has been very little understanding of the sexual aspect of marriage and this has caused distress and tension in the relationship. Nowadays, with the widespread influence of films and the internet, as well as books, the problem is often the opposite. From a young age many people are bombarded with all sorts of inappropriate images and sexual practices. This makes it even more necessary for Christians to be guided and instructed from the Bible.

In different parts of the world differences about marriage have led to a diversity of customs. Some of these customs conflict with a Christian view; others are simply variations which can fit within it. Human sinful disobedience to God has always affected marriage. It is under particular pressures in the present day. This is mainly because of the spread of secularism—that is, a view of life that leaves God and his Word completely out of the picture. Such a view is widely expressed in books, films, newspapers and the internet.

This book, however, is based on the authority of the Bible as the inspired Word of God. In doing so it follows the example of our Saviour and Lord himself, Jesus Christ, who clearly endorsed the Old Testament as the Word of God (see John 10:35; Matthew 26:29–32: Luke 24:25–27,44). And it, is written for those who themselves believe in Jesus Christ and accept the Bible as God's Word. It does not attempt to interact with those who might want to take a different view.

For us to understand what marriage is meant to be, therefore, we have to look carefully at what the Bible tells us. This is where we find guidance for all matters of Christian belief and practice. The Bible, however, is a big book. Its history covers the whole period from creation to the time of the early Christian church. It also shows to us behaviour and practices that have arisen because of human sin. It is only when we have considered everything that the Bible has to say that we can set out in full what it teaches. For this reason we shall start with a brief introduction to marriage. This will then be discussed more fully and made clearer as the book proceeds.

A very brief definition of marriage would be this: marriage

is the union of a man and a woman. It is a union that has a purpose; that purpose is for those who are married to serve God by doing his will together. They are to live for his glory. They are to serve as stewards, cultivating, preserving and using wisely the resources of the good earth God has created. In doing this, they are to develop and use the abilities that God has given them. For this to continue into the future, children have to be born, nurtured and taught. Then, after their parents' death, they carry on the task of fulfilling God's will.

So the procreation of children and the ongoing life of the family is an essential part of the meaning of marriage. It was never intended by God simply to be an opportunity for two people to become absorbed in each other. Rather, a married couple first serves their own generation and then the generations to come through the family. All this will need to be considered in greater detail later. Some married couples, for example, are not able to have children. Mankind's fall into sin in the beginning (see Genesis 3) has affected every part of life. There are many factors arising from the fall that affect marriage.

The book is set out in this way. First we look at what the Bible says about marriage, considering a number of important passages from both the Old Testament and the New Testament. Brief comments are made on each passage. These comments give some help in understanding what is being said. They show how the passages build up our knowledge of the whole subject. Do not just agree with what is written in this book without giving proper thought to what the Bible actually says, as well as the explanation. Give time to thinking through what is being said. There are also many other places in the Bible that you can refer to.

Secondly, we consider a number of practical questions relating to marriage. This includes matters like singleness, polygamy and divorce. There are problems that can arise where cultures are influenced by pagan or secular ideas. Modern life and the global influence of the mass media also mean that the same sort of problems and difficulties are arising across the world. We have to seek to live in a God-honouring way in the world as it is. Many differences of opinion among Christians about marriage go back to the pressures that they feel in their own situations. So do give careful thought to what is written here.

Finally, we consider marriage itself more closely; its blessings and its difficulties, its opportunities and its dangers, its challenges and what Christian responses should be. In many ways, this book only gives basic instruction. It is a primer, it points the way. Readers are encouraged to study the Bible carefully for themselves. Pastors and Christian leaders, in particular, need to gain a thorough understanding of all the aspects of this subject. They need to develop a thoughtful, caring, sympathetic approach as they minister to God's people.

# Part 1: Beginning with the Bible

# 1. Creation

Jesus was once asked a question about divorce (see Matthew 19:2–6). He replied by reminding his questioners of what God had done and said at the very beginning. He quoted to them from Genesis 2:24. So we too will go back to the beginning, and start in Genesis 1: 'Then God said, "Let us make man in our image, after our likeness. And let them have dominion over the fish of the sea and over the birds of the heavens and over the livestock and over all the earth and over every creeping thing that creeps on the earth." So God created man in his own image, in the image of God he created him; male and female he created them. And God blessed them. And God said to them, "Be fruitful and multiply and fill the earth and subdue it and have dominion over the fish of the sea and over the birds of the heavens and over every living thing that moves on the earth"' (verses 26–28).

When it came to creating mankind, there is a difference from all God's earlier creative acts. Before creating human beings God thought within himself and decided what he would do (verse 26). This shows three things. Firstly, the importance that he attaches to people, as compared with all other living things on earth. Secondly, mankind was to be in his image. This means that in a number of ways we reflect what God is like. This image has been spoiled by Adam's fall into sin, but it still remains (see James 3:9). Thirdly, God has a purpose in creating us. That purpose includes people having authority over all the rest of creation.

After his decision, God acted and made the first human beings. The second chapter of Genesis will show us that he first created a man and then afterwards fashioned a woman from the man. In this chapter we are told the basic facts that human beings were made in God's image and also created male and female. This shows us that though there is a sexual difference between a man and a woman, yet they are equal. Both share the same image of God. Both share authority over the rest of creation. And as verse 28 tells us, both share a task to be done for God in his world.

Having created the first humans, God's next act was to bless them (verse 28). 'To bless' here includes his joy over them. It also means his active goodness would strengthen and help them. He was dedicating them to the purpose for which he had made them. Then he gave them a commission. Firstly, they were to be fruitful and multiply and fill the earth. This came first because it was essential for the carrying out of God's ultimate purpose. Two persons were put into the earth to 'subdue it and have dominion … over every living thing that moves on the earth'. Clearly that could not be done by them alone. Human beings needed to multiply, if the task was ever to be carried out. God's first command to the man and woman was for them to engage in sexual union and bear children, so that eventually the earth might be filled. Here we see that marriage is a calling from God that belongs to the very essence of being human.

The main purpose is to 'subdue' the earth and have dominion 'over … every living thing that moves on the earth'. We learn more about what this involved in the second chapter of Genesis. In the early verses of this chapter, we are told how God formed the man from 'the dust of the earth'. The word for 'man' in the original language of the Old Testament is 'Adam', which also became the name of the first man. In verse 15 we see that the LORD God placed Adam in the garden of Eden 'to work it and keep it'. The task of 'subduing the earth' began in this garden of special beauty and fruitfulness. Adam was to care for the garden, to look after it and gather its fruits for his own use. He was called to be a steward over God's creation, maintaining it and developing it. He was God's manager, his gardener. He was to work and use the good creation of God for his own benefit and for God's glory. He had a responsibility before God to fulfil the purpose of his existence.

As Genesis 2 progresses, we come to verse 18: 'Then the LORD God said, "It is not good that the man should be alone; I will make a helper fit for him."' Among the created animals no suitable helper was found for Adam. 'So the LORD God caused a deep sleep to fall upon the man, and while he slept took one of his ribs and closed up its place with flesh. And the rib that the LORD God had taken from the man he made into a woman and brought her to the man. Then the man said, "This at last is bone of my bones and flesh of my flesh; she shall be called Woman, because she was taken out of Man." Therefore a man shall leave his father and mother and hold fast to his wife, and they shall become one flesh. And the man and his wife were both naked and were not ashamed' (verses 21–25).

As we look at this section, it is important to keep in mind what we have already seen. Adam could not fulfil the calling he had been given all alone. He needed someone to help him. Another man would have been sufficient for friendship and working together. But important though companionship is, he needed more than that. He needed someone who would become a helper and partner in fulfilling the task that God had given, but who would also enable him to be fruitful and multiply. In this way, the future would be secured.

The way God met this need shows what marriage is intended to be. The first woman was taken from the side of the first man. This indicates complete equality and co-dignity. For Adam, his wife would be part of himself, emphasising the unity that they shared. They were one flesh in two quite different senses. It was God himself who brought the woman to Adam, and by doing so he brought about the first marriage. She was a gift from God, yet she had been fashioned from her husband. They were one both by creation and by giving. When she was brought to him, Adam spoke the first love song: "This at last is bone of my bones and flesh of my flesh; she shall be called Woman, because she was taken out of Man." There is a note of joy and exultation here. Now there is someone who will be just the one that Adam needed!

What took place there in the garden is the pattern for the future. As Jesus said, 'Therefore a man shall leave his father and mother and hold fast to his wife, and they shall become one flesh' (Matthew 19:5). Three things are important in this statement. Firstly, in future a man will leave his father and mother in order to be joined to his wife. Just as God, who formed the woman from Adam's body, gave her to him, so a man, and by implication, a woman, will leave behind old relationships in order to form a new one. Secondly, a man is to hold fast to his wife. He is to be committed to her and faithful to that commitment. Once more the same holds true for the wife; though it may be that the verse shows that the man is to set an example, both in leaving and joining. Also, it may be that men are more likely to be tempted to unfaithfulness. Thirdly, they are to become one flesh. They now belong together, and this is expressed and symbolised by their union in sexual intercourse. This is an exclusive relationship, not to be shared with or intruded upon by any other.

Several important truths emerge from these passages. Firstly, while it is true that marriage brings about a wonderful bond of companionship, it is not simply a remedy for loneliness. The opposite is true. The marriage union has an outward look and this needs to be understood. Together, husband and wife take part in God's purpose of working in and caring for his creation. They are the servants of God together, but they also provide for their task to be continued in the future through the children granted to them.

Secondly, unlike what seems to have been the case with other living creatures (see Genesis 1:20–25), God began with just two human beings. This means that the human race is actually one large family. Family life and kinship are therefore very important. The blessings of family life and family loyalty and mutual help extend outwards. This sense of belonging needs to be kept. Every person is an individual. However, concentrating just on the individual—individualism—is divisive. It breeds loneliness and an uncaring attitude.

Thirdly, from the beginning it was important for the married woman to bear children. So, for some years at least, her role would be mainly in the home and with the care of growing children. This was never to be considered drudgery or burdensome. It was a wonderful privilege, and vital for fulfilling her part in the purpose of God.

Fourthly, Genesis 2 ends with these words, 'And the man and his wife were both naked and were not ashamed.' This clearly shows us that there is nothing indecent about any part of the human body. Nor is there anything wrong in the naked openness of husband and wife. However, these words also alert us to the fact that at this point sin had not entered the world. We can and should learn the basic truth about marriage from the beginning of the Bible. But now we have to live and serve God as imperfect people in a very imperfect world.

However, here is the joyous ideal. A man and a woman united together in complete harmony. Serving God in developing and using the resources of the good earth on which they live. Intelligent and creative in the ways by which they accomplish this. Loving God and living in communion with him. Loving and assisting one another; producing children for the future. These are the goals for which Christians should aim in marriage.

# 2. Marriage and the Law of Moses

God gave his law to Israel through Moses. At the centre of that law are the Ten Commandments (Exodus 20; Deuteronomy 5). There are also other laws which are found in those books and in Leviticus and Numbers. These books are together usually known as the Law of Moses. Before we look directly at this law which God gave through Moses, it is best to consider the background to the law. We will look first at what happened between creation and the giving of the law. Then we turn to the circumstances in which the law was given.

As far as we can tell, it was not very long after the creation of Adam and his wife Eve that they fell into disobedience. Their sin changed everything. Not only did evil become a power in their own hearts, but the animal creation and the earth itself was subjected to futility and bondage (Romans 8:19–22).

Immediately, their own relationship was affected. Adam blamed the woman for giving him the fruit of the tree. God said to the woman, 'Your desire shall be for your husband, and he shall rule over you' (Genesis 3:16). The exact meaning of these words is debated, but they probably mean, 'You shall desire to rule over your husband, but he will *dominate over you.*' Instead of the perfect relationship of love, trust and harmony which they had enjoyed, times of tension would come between them. In future, they would have to work at living together harmoniously. This would no longer come naturally.

For all their descendants, right down to the present day, marriage could never be the perfect relationship that it once was. When two Christians marry, it is two forgiven sinners who marry, not two perfect people. So a law became necessary and guidance had to be given. These are what we find in the Bible. By the grace of God and the work of his Spirit, Christian marriages can become more and more what they ought to be. For this, there must be mutual trust in God and a wholehearted commitment to the marriage promises. There will need to be love and prayer, and willingness on both sides to apologise and forgive when these are necessary.

When we read on in Genesis, we are saddened to see what sin does. In chapter four, we find a man with two wives. In chapter nine, we read of indecent exposure. As the book goes on there is adultery, rape, incest, prostitution, seduction, and even attempted homosexual rape. Jacob, who is the father of the nation of Israel, had children by four different women. It is a very sad picture, one which cries out for some guidance and help from God.

This was the background to the giving of the law. It was given at the time when the people of Israel were preparing to go into the land of Canaan. The last two verses of Genesis 11 and the opening verses of the next chapter show us that Abraham had settled in the land of Canaan. Reading on, it soon becomes clear that the inhabitants of the land, the Canaanites, were very evil people. God promised Abraham that he would give the land of Canaan to his descendants. This would only take place four hundred years later, when the time had come for God's judgement upon the Canaanites (Genesis 15:12–21).

This came about in the time of Moses. It was then that the descendants of Abraham, Isaac and Jacob came out of Egypt to settle in the land of Canaan. God made it very clear to the Israelites that they were to expel the Canaanites from the land because of their vile and wicked behaviour. 'Do not make yourselves unclean by any of these things, for by all these the nations I am driving out before you have become unclean, and the land became unclean, so that I punished its iniquity, and the land vomited out its inhabitants' (Leviticus 18:24–25).

The Israelites also needed to understand that they must take great care not to follow the example of the Canaanites. 'But you shall keep my statutes and my rules and do none of these abominations, either the native or the stranger who sojourns among you (for the people of the land, who were before you, did all of these abominations, so that the land became unclean), lest the land vomit you out when you make it unclean, as it vomited out the nation that was before you' (Leviticus 18:26–28). God's laws were given against the background of the terrible evils of the Canaanites. They were given to guide Israel to conduct that would be pleasing to the Lord.

*The Ten Commandments* (Exodus 20:1–17; Deuteronomy 5:1–21): We come first to the Ten Commandments. These lie at the heart of a life pleasing to God. There are three commandments which have some bearing on marriage. The fifth commandment says, 'Honour your father and your mother, that your days may be long in the land that the LORD your God is giving you' (Exodus 20:12). This is not directly about marriage but is clearly about life in the family. Children are to honour father and mother. The mother is included as well as the father; in some societies the mother has not been given equal respect with the father.

This command shows us that the authority of parents is to be recognised and respected in the home. Learning to respect authority in the home leads to a stable society. A stable and mutually respectful society will continue as such into the future. However, where authority is not recognised, rulers tend to enforce the law by power. This has often led to dictatorship. The alternative to this is divisiveness which can lead to the break-up of a nation. Paul shows the continuing importance of this command in Ephesians 6:1–3: 'Children, obey your parents in the Lord, for this is right. "Honour your father and mother" (this is the first commandment with a promise), "that it may go well with you and that you may live long in the land."' Marriage and family life are vital to a healthy society.

The seventh commandment says, 'You shall not commit adultery' (Exodus 20:14). This is a commandment protecting the marriage union from unfaithfulness. It is simple and direct, without any qualification. This command includes all other forms of sexual behaviour that lie beyond the proper sexual union of marriage. Fornication is sexual union outside of marriage, just as adultery is. In 1 Timothy 1:8–11 Paul refers to the right use of the law. He mentions how several of the commandments are broken, showing extreme forms of such disobedience. He says that the law was made for 'the sexually immoral, [and] men who practice homosexuality'. Here he is referring to the seventh commandment.

The last commandment gets to the root of disobedience, the heart. It speaks of the danger of unrestrained desire for what belongs to a neighbour, the command including, 'You shall not

covet your neighbour's wife' (Exodus 20:17). It is not enough to
abstain from actually committing sexual sin. The desire, and
what encourages and inflames that desire, must be dealt with.
We cannot always avoid what we see, nor can we always stop
thoughts arising in our minds, but at that point we can say, 'No'.
We are to reject what we know to be sinful, both in thought
and deed.

These three commands are not the only instructions about
marriage given to the Israelites at that time. There are many
others, and we need to look at some of the most important of
these. As we do so, we have to realise that the Israelites were
inevitably influenced by what happened around them at that
time. These instructions may not be directly applicable to most
societies today, but there are still similarities to each of them
in some cultures. Such guidance can be helpful in considering
principles for action, even where there is no direct application.
We look at them in the order in which they occur in the Bible.

*Exodus 21:7–11*: 'When a man sells his daughter as a slave, she
shall not go out as the male slaves do. If she does not please her
master, who has designated her for himself, then he shall let her
be redeemed. He shall have no right to sell her to a foreign people,
since he has broken faith with her. If he designates her for his
son, he shall deal with her as with a daughter. If he takes another
wife to himself, he shall not diminish her food, her clothing, or
her marital rights. And if he does not do these three things for
her, she shall go out for nothing, without payment of money.'

Immediately after the Ten Commandments, we find
instructions given about slaves. The form of slavery that then
existed within Israel was actually a way of relieving poverty. If a

family fell on hard times, members of the family could be taken into the service of another family. Such persons would work for the master and his household for seven years. The 'slave' was to be treated properly and provided for, and then at the end of seven years he or she had to be set free to return home.

The case might arise where an unmarried woman became the slave of an unmarried man and the two married. Suppose, however, that the man later also decided to marry a free woman. In Israel, polygamous marriages did sometimes take place. In these circumstances the slave wife might be treated badly. So verses ten and eleven say: 'If he takes another wife to himself, he shall not diminish her food, her clothing, or her marital rights. And if he does not do these three things for her, she shall go out for nothing, without payment of money.' 'Marital rights' here would include continuing sexual union.

This was a way of dealing with a situation which would not arise if the creation pattern of marriage was closely followed. It provided for a situation where that pattern had been disregarded. It indicates that any husband has responsibilities to his wife that he ought to fulfil, even, as in this case, if he takes a second wife. There are obligations that every husband has to his wife which, if he fails to carry out, must call the marriage itself into question. We shall see later how this instruction can still help us today.

*Leviticus 18*: This chapter falls into four sections, and as it is a long chapter it will not be quoted here. Verses one to five are concerned to tell the people of Israel that they must not follow the example either of the Egyptians or the Canaanites in their behaviour. They must follow the rules that God gives them.

The longest section, verses six to eighteen, forbids the marriage of close relatives. These are both blood relatives, and in some cases, relatives by marriage. It is interesting to remember that Abraham's wife Sarah was the daughter of his father, though not of his mother (Genesis 20:12). Also Jacob was married to two sisters (Genesis 29:21–30). Neither of these marriages would have been legitimate under the rules given later in Leviticus 18.

The third section, verses 19–23, includes forbidding same-sex union and bestiality. These are listed along with child-sacrifice as abominations and perversions. The fourth section, verses 24–30, explains the reasons for the prohibitions in this chapter. It was the things listed here which were unclean in the sight of the LORD and resulted in the Canaanites being driven out of the land.

*Leviticus 21:7:* 'They [the priests] shall not marry a prostitute or a woman who has been defiled, neither shall they marry a woman divorced from her husband, for the priest is holy to his God.'

*Leviticus 21:13–15:* 'And he [the high priest] shall take a wife in her virginity. A widow, or a divorced woman, or a woman who has been defiled, or a prostitute, these he shall not marry. But he shall take as his wife a virgin of his own people, that he may not profane his offspring among his people, for I am the Lord who sanctifies him.'

These verses come in a section which gives instructions concerning the priests. Verse 7 tells us that a priest may not marry a woman who is a prostitute, or who has been defiled, nor divorced from her husband. The other verses, speaking of the high priest, repeat these prohibitions but add that he may not marry a widow either. The clear implication of these verses is that an ordinary Israelite was free to marry such women, including those who had been divorced.

*Deuteronomy 21:10–14*: 'When you go out to war against your enemies, and the LORD your God gives them into your hand and you take them captive, and you see among the captives a beautiful woman, and you desire to take her to be your wife, and you bring her home to your house, she shall shave her head and pare her nails. And she shall take off the clothes in which she was captured and shall remain in your house and lament her father and her mother a full month. After that you may go in to her and be her husband, and she shall be your wife. But if you no longer delight in her, you shall let her go where she wants. But you shall not sell her for money, nor shall you treat her as a slave, since you have humiliated her.'

This small section is about an Israelite man who marries a woman captured in warfare. In such a case he cannot simply treat her as the spoils of war and act just as he wishes. She shall be given a month to lament the deaths of her parents—these are assumed. So she is to be treated thoughtfully and kindly and given new clothes. After the month they can be married. She is never to be treated as a slave nor sold for money, but she can be divorced and then allowed to go where she wishes. This is obviously very different from what must have often taken place in pagan nations.

*Deuteronomy 22:13–21*: These verses show that in Israel, evidence of a bride's virginity was kept by her parents in case any accusation of fornication was made against her. The rest of the chapter is also about sexual morality and marriage.

*Deuteronomy 24:1–4*: 'When a man takes a wife and marries her, if then she finds no favour in his eyes because he has found some indecency in her, and he writes her a certificate of divorce and puts it in her hand and sends her out of his house, and she departs out of his house, and if she goes and becomes another man's wife, and the latter man hates her and writes her a certificate of divorce and puts it in her hand and sends her out of his house, or if the latter man dies, who took her to be his wife, then her former husband, who sent her away, may not take her again to be his wife, after she has been defiled, for that is an abomination before the LORD. And you shall not bring sin upon the land that the LORD your God is giving you for an inheritance.'

This passage is about divorce, which took place at times in Israel. Several elements here are vital to understanding divorce in Bible days. Firstly, divorce was an act of the husband, not of the state or any official. There was no provision for a wife to divorce her husband, but in the economic circumstances of those days this would have been a very unlikely event. Secondly, he had to give a certificate to the wife he was divorcing. This could be very brief, but the point was that a second potential husband would know that she was not simply an immoral woman.

Thirdly, a divorce was final once the woman had remarried. There was to be no divorcing in a fit of anger and then perhaps deciding to take her back later on. Fourthly, the translation says of the husband, 'if then she finds no favour in his eyes because he has found some indecency in her'. This is the reason given for the divorce. The Jewish teachers did not agree among themselves about the significance of the words 'some indecency'. Modern scholars are not really sure of its meaning either. Possibly it simply means 'something that upsets him' or words to that effect.

No-one divorces for no reason at all. We must realise that this provision did not actually command or even approve divorce. What it did was to regulate divorce and provided some protection for the woman involved. People in Israel were divorcing, so God provided help to lessen its effect. Sadly, people are still divorcing.

The Roman Catholic Church and some other Christians believe that marriage is indissoluble. This means that the union still remains binding, even if divorce takes place, and so neither person ought to marry again. However, this passage shows that this cannot be the case. Here, a man who has divorced his wife and then married again cannot resume the first marriage, if he divorces a second time. If, however, his original marriage was indissoluble, then this would be the proper thing to do.

*Deuteronomy 24:5 (see also 20:5–7):* 'When a man is newly married, he shall not go out with the army or be liable for any other public duty. He shall be free at home one year to be happy with his wife whom he has taken.'

An opportunity for a married couple to settle down together was an important part of Israel's law. No newly married man was to be sent on any public duty for the first year of marriage. Such a period of time would help to cement their relationship. It gave them an opportunity to learn about each other and to establish a harmonious life together.

*Deuteronomy 25:5–10:* 'If brothers dwell together, and one of them dies and has no son, the wife of the dead man shall not be married outside the family to a stranger. Her husband's brother shall go in to her and take her as his wife and perform the duty of a husband's brother to her. And the first son whom she bears shall succeed to the name of his dead brother, that his name may not be blotted out of Israel. And if the man does not wish to take his brother's wife, then his brother's wife shall go up to the gate to the elders and say, "My husband's brother refuses to perpetuate his brother's name in Israel; he will not perform the duty of a husband's brother to me." Then the elders of his city shall call him and speak to him, and if he persists, saying, "I do not wish to take her," then his brother's wife shall go up to him in the presence of the elders and pull his sandal off his foot and spit in his face. And she shall answer and say, "So shall it be done to the man who does not build up his brother's house." And the name of his house shall be called in Israel, "The house of him who had his sandal pulled off.'"

These verses speak of what is known as Levirate marriage. The procedure is quite clear. If brothers live together—presumably that means close to each other—and one dies without a son and heir, then the other brother is to marry the widow so that there she can bear an heir for her dead husband. It does not say that the brother who takes the widow has to be single. Presumably if he was already married, she would become a second wife and would continue to be so treated even after an heir had been born.

We should not think that this Old Testament provision needs to be carried out by Christians today. However, there are still some areas in the world where a similar procedure sometimes takes place. It is likely to be phased out as time passes, but it cannot be simply condemned. This provision does underline the importance of the wider family. Responsibility and care should go beyond the single family to the wider family of close relatives.

Another important Old Testament passage: Proverbs 31:10–31

'An excellent wife who can find? She is far more precious than jewels.

The heart of her husband trusts in her, and he will have no lack of gain.

She does him good, and not harm, all the days of her life.

She seeks wool and flax, and works with willing hands.

She is like the ships of the merchant; she brings her food from afar.

She rises while it is yet night and provides food for her household and portions for her maidens.

She considers a field and buys it; with the fruit of her hands she plants a vineyard.

She dresses herself with strength and makes her arms strong.

She perceives that her merchandise is profitable. Her lamp does not go out at night.

She puts her hands to the distaff, and her hands hold the spindle.

She opens her hand to the poor and reaches out her hands to the needy.

She is not afraid of snow for her household, for all her household are clothed in scarlet.

She makes bed coverings for herself; her clothing is fine linen and purple.

Her husband is known in the gates when he sits among the elders of the land.

She makes linen garments and sells them; she delivers sashes to the merchant.

Strength and dignity are her clothing, and she laughs at the time to come.

She opens her mouth with wisdom, and the teaching of kindness is on her tongue.

She looks well to the ways of her household and does not eat the bread of idleness.

Her children rise up and call her blessed; her husband also, and he praises her:

"Many women have done excellently, but you surpass them all."

Charm is deceitful, and beauty is vain, but a woman who fears the LORD is to be praised.

Give her of the fruit of her hands, and let her works praise her in the gates.'

This is a remarkable passage in many ways, and is often overlooked. It is, of course, expressed in terms of Old Testament times. It probably dates from round about the period of Solomon because the times were evidently prosperous. It is an ideal, but the expectations here are very significant. While the picture clearly describes a happy home life and care of children, it goes far beyond that. Here is a business woman, who may even travel far to purchase what she needs. She not only buys, she sells also. She is diligent and takes care of the needy. She is wise and fears the LORD; she is able to teach kindness and goodness to others. This is the biblical picture and it gives a warrant for women whose lives may be centred around the home, especially when children are young, but whose activities and interests and influence extend far beyond.

# 3. Marriage in the New Testament

## The teaching of Jesus

M*atthew 5:27–32*: 'You have heard that it was said, "You shall not commit adultery." But I say to you that everyone who looks at a woman with lustful intent has already committed adultery with her in his heart. If your right eye causes you to sin, tear it out and throw it away. For it is better that you lose one of your members than that your whole body be thrown into hell. And if your right hand causes you to sin, cut it off and throw it away. For it is better that you lose one of your members than that your whole body go into hell. It was also said, "Whoever divorces his wife, let him give her a certificate of divorce." But I say to you that everyone who divorces his wife, except on the ground of sexual immorality, makes her commit adultery. And whoever marries a divorced woman commits adultery.'

These words of the Lord Jesus are often divided into two sections. For example, the English Standard Version does this. Its heading for verses 27–30 is 'Lust', and for verses 31–32 is 'Divorce'. However, a closer look shows us that the subject is actually adultery. There were two ways in which some men in those days broke the command against adultery, even though they imagined that they kept it. Men were breaking the command firstly by a lustful look and secondly by their practice of divorce. It may be that often these two were related. The lustful look led to a man divorcing his wife so that he could then marry the woman after whom he lusted.

The look is described as a look with a 'lustful intent'. This links with the tenth commandment, 'You shall not covet your neighbour's wife'. It is not just seeing someone very attractive in passing, it goes beyond that. It is what happens in the mind when a man sees a woman; how he reacts to what he has seen, and what further thoughts and desires he allows within himself. In the society in which Jesus lived what he says would apply almost entirely to men. In some present societies women also look at men with 'lustful intent'.

Verses 31–32 are concerned with an abuse of the procedure for divorce set out in Deuteronomy. We will start by looking at the exception: 'But I say to you that everyone who divorces his wife, *except on the ground of sexual immorality.*' Jesus here says that it is legitimate to divorce on the ground of 'sexual immorality'. We might ask what he meant by that and why he didn't use the word 'adultery'. In the Mosaic legislation an adulterer was to be stoned to death (see, for example, Deuteronomy 22:22). However, there is no record in the Old Testament of any person who actually suffered this punishment. King David committed adultery but it does not seem that death was ever considered for him or for Bathsheba.

It seems clear that, as time went by, death was replaced by divorce as the punishment (see, for example, Jeremiah 3:8; Isaiah 50:1). This is confirmed by what we read of Joseph in Matthew 1 concerning Mary, the mother of Jesus. 'Now the birth of Jesus Christ took place in this way. When his mother Mary had been betrothed to Joseph, before they came together she was found to be with child from the Holy Spirit. And her husband Joseph, being a just man and unwilling to put her to shame, resolved to divorce her quietly' (v.18–19). According to Deuteronomy 22:23–24 death was the punishment for a betrothed virgin who betrayed her promise to her future husband by engaging in sexual intercourse with someone else. However, Joseph was simply resolved to divorce her, and to do it quietly, to spare her as much as possible.

In Matthew 5, our Lord acknowledges that the sin that demanded the death penalty in the past had now become the ground for divorce. But he spoke of 'sexual immorality' rather than 'adultery'. In the law there were also two other sexual sins that required the death penalty, homosexual behaviour and bestiality (Leviticus 18:22–23). So the best way to understand our Lord's use of the word translated as 'sexual immorality' is this. He is teaching that those sexual sins which deserved the death penalty under the Old Covenant are now the grounds for divorce.

We must remember what we have already seen from Deuteronomy 24. Divorce in Israel was the act of the husband, not the act of the state or any third party. This leads us to consider this sentence: 'But I say to you that everyone who divorces his wife, except on the ground of sexual immorality, makes her commit adultery'. What Jesus is saying is this. Divorce is allowed on the ground of sexual sin, but where a man divorces his wife on other grounds, he causes her to commit adultery. But how does a man do this by divorcing his wife?

It is clear that Jesus must be concluding that the ex-wife will marry again. Indeed, in those days she would almost certainly need to do so. Opportunities for single women to make a living were severely limited. So the husband, because he had divorced her, was forcing her into a new marriage which really ought not to have taken place. Technically it was adulterous. The original language is very strong here. Literally it is something like 'he makes her to be adulterated'. It is clear that the blame for this belongs to the divorcing husband and not the woman who remarries. Obviously, this also means that the man she marries also technically commits adultery. The purpose that Jesus had in view here was not to prevent such second marriages from taking place. What he wanted to do was to put a stop to the casual and unjustified divorces which caused them.

We can see from this passage that our Lord gives one ground for legitimate divorce, serious sexual sin. In such cases, he also permits remarriage upon divorce. However, in cases where a person has been divorced on unjustifiable grounds, the divorcer bears the responsibility—and the guilt for the subsequent remarriage of the one whom he divorced.

*Matthew 19:3–12*: 'And Pharisees came up to him and tested him by asking, "Is it lawful to divorce one's wife for any cause?" He answered, "Have you not read that he who created them from the beginning made them male and female, and said, 'Therefore a man shall leave his father and his mother and hold fast to his wife, and they shall become one flesh'? So they are no longer two but one flesh. What therefore God has joined together, let not man separate." They said to him, "Why then did Moses command one to give a certificate of divorce and to send her away?" He said to them, "Because of your hardness of heart Moses allowed you to divorce your wives, but from the beginning it was not so. And I say to you: whoever divorces his wife, except for sexual immorality, and marries another, commits adultery."

'The disciples said to him, "If such is the case of a man with his wife, it is better not to marry." But he said to them, "Not everyone can receive this saying, but only those to whom it is given. For there are eunuchs who have been so from birth, and there are eunuchs who have been made eunuchs by men, and there are eunuchs who have made themselves eunuchs for the sake of the kingdom of heaven. Let the one who is able to receive this receive it."'

This passage confirms what we saw in chapter 5. Jesus says, 'And I say to you: whoever divorces his wife, except for sexual immorality, and marries another, commits adultery.' The only ground for divorce is sexual immorality, and those who divorce for any other reason and marry again are guilty of adultery. In this passage, no mention is made of the remarriage of a person who has been wrongly divorced. But we have already seen in the earlier chapter that the fault for the remarriage of a wronged partner lies with the one who divorces that partner.

More importantly, in this passage Jesus takes the Pharisees back to creation. He adds this significant warning, 'What therefore God has joined together, let not man separate.' From this we see that marriage is a divine institution. God not only authorises marriage but it is he who also joins the couple together. This applies to all marriages, whether or not they take place in a Christian act of worship. Though a marriage may take place before the civil authorities, it is still a divinely instituted union. The warning, however, is very important. Divorce separates those whom God has joined together. No-one should divorce unless there are real and serious grounds for doing so.

Not unnaturally, the Pharisees asked why, if marriage is God joining two people together, Moses permitted divorce. The answer was simply this, 'Because of your hardness of heart.' Significantly, Jesus did not say, 'Because of their hardness of heart' referring to the people of Moses' day. Rather, he said, 'Because of your hardness of heart'. The Pharisees were showing exactly the same attitude of heart as the people of the past had done. Israel was born as a nation in the midst of pagan peoples, whose lifestyle was far from the ways of God. The Mosaic permission of divorce, therefore, regulated and kept divorce within bounds, but it was never the ideal that God intended.

There is, however, one further point that must be mentioned. In English, and perhaps in many other languages, 'divorce' is a technical word with a specific and legal meaning. In the New Testament the words translated 'divorce' are not like that. Three different words are used which mean 'to put away', 'to separate oneself from' and 'to send away'. The focus is not on a legal procedure, but rather on the act of putting away a marriage partner. This means that if a husband or wife simply goes off and abandons the other, that is divorce. It is 'separating oneself from' the other.

These two passages from Matthew show clearly that Jesus was concerned to prevent divorce from taking place. While he acknowledged that it could happen, this was not what God intended at the beginning. Christians must do all they can to make marriages continue harmoniously. It is part of the responsibility of pastors, not only to instruct but also to counsel and help those in their churches who get into difficulty in their marriages.

## Instructions in the Letters

*1 Corinthians 6:12–20*: "'All things are lawful for me,' but not all things are helpful. "All things are lawful for me," but I will not be enslaved by anything. "Food is meant for the stomach and the stomach for food"—and God will destroy both one and the other. The body is not meant for sexual immorality, but for the Lord, and the Lord for the body. And God raised the Lord and will also raise us up by his power. Do you not know that your bodies are members of Christ? Shall I then take the members of Christ and make them members of a prostitute? Never! Or do you not know that he who is joined to a prostitute becomes one body with her? For, as it is written, "The two will become one flesh." But he who is joined to the Lord becomes one spirit with him. Flee from sexual immorality. Every other sin a person commits is outside the body, but the sexually immoral person sins against his own body. Or do you not know that your body is a temple of the Holy Spirit within you, whom you have from God? You are not your own, for you were bought with a price. So glorify God in your body.'

*1 Corinthians 7:1–5*: 'Now concerning the matters about which you wrote: "It is good for a man not to have sexual relations with a woman." But because of the temptation to sexual immorality, each man should have his own wife and each woman her own husband. The husband should give to his wife her conjugal rights, and likewise the wife to her husband. For the wife does not have authority over her own body, but the husband does. Likewise the husband does not have authority over his own body, but the wife does. Do not deprive one another, except perhaps by agreement for a limited time, that you may devote yourselves to prayer; but then come together again, so that Satan may not tempt you because of your lack of self-control.'

The section from chapter 6 provides the background for the instructions in the second paragraph, the beginning of chapter 7. Chapter 6 indicates that some, at least, in Corinth were indulging in sexual relations outside of marriage. Corinth was noted for its immorality, so this may have been a habit from before conversion. It may also be because some of the women in Corinth were saying, as Paul quotes, 'It is good for a man not to have sexual relations with a woman.' Paul does not deny this; it is clearly right for those who are single, but it is not right for those who are married. The rest of the passage makes this clear. Husbands and wives must recognise the needs and desires of the other. When Paul says 'each man should have his own wife and each woman her own husband' he is not saying that everyone should be married. He means that each man should keep himself to his own wife. The wife should also keep herself for her husband. We now look at the next verses in this chapter.

*1 Corinthians 7:6–16*: 'Now as a concession, not a command, I say this. I wish that all were as I myself am. But each has his own gift from God, one of one kind and one of another. To the unmarried and the widows I say that it is good for them to remain single as I am. But if they cannot exercise self-control, they should marry. For it is better to marry than to be aflame with passion. To the married I give this charge (not I, but the Lord): the wife should not separate from her husband (but if she does, she should remain unmarried or else be reconciled to her husband), and the husband should not divorce his wife. To the rest I say (I, not the Lord) that if any brother has a wife who is an unbeliever, and she consents to live with him, he should not divorce her. If any woman has a husband who is an unbeliever, and he consents to live with her, she should not divorce him. For the unbelieving husband is made holy because of his wife, and the unbelieving wife is made holy because of her husband. Otherwise your children would be unclean, but as it is, they are holy. But if the unbelieving partner separates, let it be so. In such cases the brother or sister is not enslaved. God has called you to peace. Wife, how do you know whether you will save your husband? Husband, how do you know whether you will save your wife?'

The background here is not the Old Testament, but the Greek and Roman culture in Corinth. In this culture, both men and women could divorce the other. As in Israel, however, this was not a matter of getting a divorce from the state. It was something either the husband or wife could do. Nor was there any need for a certificate. It was generally either a matter of the husband sending his wife away, or the wife going away of her own will. As we have already seen, the words which are generally translated by 'divorce' in English are not technical words at all. They simply mean, 'send away', 'put away', or 'separate from'. In the Old Testament, a man could put away his wife. In the Roman culture of New Testament days, either partner could do the same to the other.

Notice that Paul says that a wife who separates from her husband should remain 'unmarried' (vv.10–11). In other words, the marriage no longer exists; it has finished. Paul does, however, leave open the possibility of the marriage being reinstated. The case here does not mention any adultery on the part of the husband. If that had taken place, according to the teaching of

Jesus which we have seen, remarriage to another man would be an option.

From verse 12 onwards, the case of someone married to an unbeliever is considered. It would not be unusual for one partner to be converted but for the other to remain in unbelief. In this case, Paul counsels believers to remain with the partner. But if the unbeliever wishes to leave and there is no peace in the home, then the right thing is to let him or her go. In this case, it is the unbeliever who leaves the Christian. This would mean that the Christian was free to remarry. The Christian is not to believe he or she is still 'enslaved' or 'in bondage' to the other. The marriage bond has been broken.

*Ephesians 5:22–33*: 'Wives, submit to your own husbands, as to the Lord. For the husband is the head of the wife even as Christ is the head of the church, his body, and is himself its Saviour. Now as the church submits to Christ, so also wives should submit in everything to their husbands. Husbands, love your wives, as Christ loved the church and gave himself up for her, that he might sanctify her, having cleansed her by the washing of water with the word, so that he might present the church to himself in splendour, without spot or wrinkle or any such thing, that she might be holy and without blemish. In the same way husbands should love their wives as their own bodies. He who loves his wife loves himself. For no one ever hated his own flesh, but nourishes and cherishes it, just as Christ does the church, because we are members of his body. "Therefore a man shall leave his father and mother and hold fast to his wife, and the two shall become one flesh." This mystery is profound, and I am saying that it refers to Christ and the church. However, let each one of you love his wife as himself, and let the wife see that she respects her husband.'

This is one of the most important passages about marriage in the whole Bible. It lifts our whole understanding of marriage to a different level by using the picture of the relationship between Christ and the church. This makes the passage very challenging. It points us to the most intimate love relationship of all. There is nothing which so exalts God's gift of marriage as this passage does.

The passage should be read as a whole. We should allow all it says to make its impression upon us. It would be quite wrong just to pick out certain sentences, perhaps those which suited us, and concentrate on these. As you can see, this passage builds on the picture in Genesis. However, it goes far beyond it, bringing marriage into the context of redemption through Jesus Christ. Two unions are brought before us. There is first the union spoken of in Genesis. A man is to 'hold fast', or 'stick close', to his wife. They become one flesh—the husband is to think of his wife as part of himself. The second union is union with Christ. All believers are joined to Christ by the Holy Spirit and so they are also joined to each other in the church. The church's union with Jesus Christ becomes the pattern for the marriage relationship. Both wife and husband are to think of their relationship to each other in those terms. That is the way to true peace and joy together.

The two key commands—and they are commands—are these: 'Wives, submit to your own husbands ... as the church submits to Christ' and 'Husbands, love your wives, as Christ loved the church.' The fact that wives are addressed first probably arises from verse 21: 'submitting to one another out of reverence for

Christ'. Christians are typically to submit to each other. They have learned from Christ to put the interests and welfare of others before their own desires or preferences. A particular application of that attitude is to be seen in the marriage relationship, on the part of the wife.

Because Christ loved the church and gave himself for it, he has become the head of the church. Apart from his self-giving there would have been no church. The members of the church have also, in response to his self-giving, given themselves to him. The church looks to him as its head and knows it can do so safely. His overwhelming love to it has already been seen. He will always guide and lead his church with love and wisdom. In times of uncertainty and difficulty, the church relies on its head and submits itself to him. It leaves its dilemmas and problems in his hands and looks for his guidance and help in sorting them out. Meanwhile, it gets on with doing what it knows will please him. Christ will never simply order his church around. He will never harm or abandon it. Christ wants his church to grow and flourish and fulfil its calling, using the gifts he bestows upon it.

In marriage, the man gives himself to the woman and takes her to be part of himself. He is to love her as his own body, strengthening and loving her, just as Christ does the church. In times of great difficulty he will take the responsibility. This means he will take the hard decisions and accept the responsibility for what happens as a result. He will protect his wife when this is necessary. He will never order her around, harm her or abandon her. He wants her to grow and flourish as a person, and use all the gifts she has been given. He wants to encourage and help her to fulfil her calling as a wife, and—in most cases—as a mother too.

Here, however, is the difficulty. We are all sinners. Even though we have been saved from our sins and brought into the church, sin remains in our hearts and we live in an evil world. Growing up as unconverted people in a world of wrong attitudes and behaviour, we learn all sorts of wrong attitudes and behaviour ourselves. Conversion itself does not make us perfect. It begins a process that only reaches perfection when we are glorified after death, or at the return of Jesus. In addition, the Fall into sin has introduced illness and disability and many other similar problems into the world.

All this means that marriage, like everything else, can never be just as it was before the disobedience of Adam and Eve. This is why Paul, in this passage, has to urge its readers to live in the marriage bond as Christians should. Marriage is a great blessing from God, but it will never be perfect. It requires understanding and effort on both sides. Because of illness and weakness, sometimes a wife has to take more responsibility than would normally be the case. Moreover, most marriages will end with one partner being widowed. We shall return to more principles for marriage later. Before that, we will consider a number of practical and important matters that must be taken into account as we think about marriage.

# Part 2: Practical Questions for Today

In this part of the book, we look at several important practical issues. These are all related to the subject of marriage. It is better to consider these individually, in turn, and then the positive explanation of marriage will come in the third section.

# 4. Singleness

Every person begins life unmarried. In the vast majority of cases, people grow up in a family, often with one or more other children. Many people who have been married also end life as singles, after the death of their partner. Some never marry and remain single all their lives. Many of these would have wished to be married but this never happened. How are we to think about singleness?

In ancient cultures like those at the time of Old Testament Israel, and in Israel herself, it was unusual to find single people. This is still the case in some parts of the world. In those days, marriage was almost essential for everyone. It was often arranged between families and sometimes a man would have several wives. Single women would have to remain in the family home and be provided for by the father; so it was in his interest to see her married if at all possible.

Nowadays, in western and westernised societies many more people live single lives. This is the result of increased social mobility, the weakening of family ties and a greater emphasis on the individual. In these countries singleness is found particularly among Christian women. This is because in many countries the percentage of women among Christian believers is greater than that of men. Christians are generally taught not to marry unbelievers (this will be considered in the next section). Christian women, who would have been glad to marry and have a family, remain single, but may often find it difficult to accept this. They may also sometimes find attitudes toward marriage, and the teaching given on marriage in churches, upsetting and insensitive to their condition.

We cannot guess at what conditions would have been like if Adam and Eve had not sinned. Nor can we assume that singleness only arises because of what they did. We do not read of many people in the Bible who were single, but there is one great example. Jesus himself remained single. He served his Father and fulfilled his ministry faithfully as a single man. His life shines out as a model of singleness to the glory of God. The apostle Paul was also single (1 Corinthians 7:6), though it is possible he may have been a widower. Mary and Martha in the Gospels also seem to have been single. Mary the mother of Jesus appears to have been widowed by the time Jesus began his ministry.

In the present day, numbers of Christian women and some men live single lives. Pastors and elders need to be sensitive to the feelings and struggles that these may experience. They should also encourage a right attitude among the married members of the church. Singleness, or celibacy as it is also known, is shown in the Bible to be a God-given calling for some people. Jesus spoke, not just of those born as eunuchs or made eunuchs, but he says: 'There are eunuchs who have made themselves eunuchs for the sake of the kingdom of heaven' (Matthew 19:12). Paul also says: 'I wish that all were as I myself am, but each has his own gift from God, one of one kind and one of another. To the unmarried and the widows I say that it is good for them to remain single as I am. But if they cannot exercise self-control, they should marry. For it is better to marry than to be aflame with passion'(1 Corinthians 7:7–9).

Single people are not to be made to feel that there is something wrong with them, nor are they to be patronised. They need to be valued for who they are and enabled to serve within the church. When the principles of marriage are taught, it is vital to remember the needs of the unmarried, too. All Christians can serve the interests of the kingdom of heaven and glorify God. In some circumstances single people can serve Christ better than those who are married. They usually do not have the same home ties. They can be more flexible and are able to move to other places more easily.

It is also important to remember the importance of friendship and Christian fellowship. Marriage was never intended for two people to retreat into a private relationship. Nor is singleness intended to be a lonely life of isolation. Singles are actually in a better position to make a wide circle of friends, and they should be encouraged to do so: 'A friend loves at all times, and a brother is born for adversity' (Proverbs 17:17).

# 5. Marrying in the Lord?

Should Christians only marry Christians? In the Old Testament the Israelites were not to marry the people of Canaan: 'You shall not intermarry with them, giving your daughters to their sons or taking their daughters for your sons, for they would turn away your sons from following me, to serve other gods. Then the anger of the LORD would be kindled against you, and he would destroy you quickly' (Deuteronomy 7:3–4). However, this did not prevent Salmon marrying the Canaanite Rahab; nor Boaz marrying Ruth, a Moabitess (Matthew 1:5). Both of these women had shown faith in the LORD, of course. Much later, Ezra was appalled at the way many Israelites had married wives from 'the peoples of the lands' (see Ezra 9 and 10, especially 9:1–5). The Old Testament makes us realise that marriage between God's people and unbelievers can have serious consequences for faith and holiness.

The New Testament does not say much on the subject. There are two main passages. 2 Corinthians 6:14 says: 'Do not be unequally yoked with unbelievers.' This seems clear, but we must realise that the whole passage down to 7:1 shows that marriage is not the main subject that Paul has in mind. What Paul was referring to was taking part in feasts in pagan temples. These feasts were often associated with trade guilds. However, 6:14 does lay down a principle which many Christians believe should also apply to such a close 'yoke' as marriage.

1 Corinthians 7:39–40 says: 'A wife is bound to her husband as long as he lives. But if her husband dies, she is free to be married to whom she wishes, only in the Lord. Yet in my judgment she is happier if she remains as she is. And I think that I too have the Spirit of God.' So a widow is free to remarry, but 'only in the Lord'. This seems decisive, for it is difficult to believe that there is one rule for widows and another for those marrying for the first time.

It is usually pastors who take marriage services and many have found that the issue is not, in practice, quite as clear as it seems from these verses. There are many questions and difficulties. What does a pastor do in the following circumstances? One of the couple wishing to be married has been brought up in a church. He or she attends regularly, does not doubt any of the truths of the gospel, but has never made a profession of faith. In Baptist churches, this would mean never having been baptized. The other person is clearly a professing believer. Some people, as we know, struggle very much with assurance and may never have committed themselves in baptism or membership for that reason. Does that mean they should not be able to marry a baptized believer?

Or consider this case. A person has been baptized, or perhaps made a clear profession of faith in some other way. However, the regularity of his or her attendance at worship, and perhaps other behaviour, raise doubts about the reality of faith. Or again, sometimes, even with truly Christian couples, the woman may be already pregnant. Should a pastor refuse to marry a couple in that case? Yet marriage is just what ought to take place in such circumstances. Another difficulty arises if an unconverted couple are engaged and one of them is converted before their marriage. Should he or she break the commitment already made, or should the marriage go ahead?

Some of these questions particularly arise because marriage often takes place in a church service, and so has to be arranged with the pastor. Not all Christians, however, have believed that marriage should take place with a service. There is nothing in the Bible that definitely says so. Sometimes a couple will get married outside of church in order to avoid a problem with the pastor and church. In cases like that, it may be thought that church discipline should be used, but that may not be the wisest course.

All these factors mean that this can be a very difficult area. It is best for pastors to be as charitable as possible in these sorts of circumstances. To marry two people in a church service simply means that their marriage explicitly takes place in the presence of God and is accompanied with prayer and the Word of God. Ultimately, the decision to get married, and the responsibility that goes with it, rests with the couple themselves.

It is important to realise that pastors and elders must not copy the authoritarianism which is so often found in the world. Peter's words are always important: 'So I exhort the elders among you, as a fellow elder and a witness of the sufferings of Christ, as well as a partaker in the glory that is going to be revealed: shepherd the flock of God that is among you, exercising oversight, not under compulsion, but willingly, as God would have you; not for shameful gain, but eagerly; not domineering over those in your charge, but being examples to the flock. And when the chief Shepherd appears, you will receive the unfading crown of glory' (1 Peter 5:1–4).

# 6. Education

It is the responsibility of the church to teach biblical principles to its members and those who come under its influence, in this case principles concerning marriage. The main responsibility for this falls on those who minister the Word of God, usually a pastor or elders. However, it is important to realise that this teaching will then be passed on within families. It may also sometimes be taught directly to men and women in the church, possibly separately, and may be given to younger people and children in youth meetings and Sunday School. Other leaders and teachers within the church will teach such groups. This teaching will tend to mould the outlook and behaviour of church members.

It is vital, therefore, for pastors and elders in particular to gain a good understanding of the relevant Bible teaching. If possible, they should read books that are more detailed than this one. They will also need carefully to think through those areas where Christians themselves differ in their understanding of Scripture. They need to consider thoughtfully whether the understanding they have gained from their own culture or background agrees with Scripture or needs to be revised. It is important for them to be aware of the influences and pressures that their congregations are under; especially the influences on those who are young. In all this, they need to guard their own minds and hearts, remembering that they too can be tempted. Far too many Christian leaders have fallen into sexual sin.

It is possible in the regular preaching of God's Word to speak frankly and openly where the passage requires it. In times past, it is likely that pastors too often passed over difficult passages in order to avoid embarrassment. It is also clear, though, that there are some things which need to be taught and understood that should not be said in public worship. Parents need to understand that it is their responsibility to speak factually and sensitively to their children from an early age, especially on matters of sex. Generally, this will be best done in answer to questions. It is particularly necessary to do so because sex education is increasingly given at school, and to very young children. Such teaching may often be far from what parents want their children to be taught. It is the responsibility of the leadership in the church to give parents the guidance and information that they need to respond to this in the home.

Many churches reach beyond church families to other young people. These can be given careful teaching, appropriate to age and cultural background. It needs to be done with wisdom, however, because the home background may be far from being what would be normal in Christian families. Children easily resent criticism of their parents, quite rightly. It is quite wrong to encourage a rebellious attitude, especially if you can see its beginnings. Always consider the young people whom you will be teaching and what their background is. Never simply follow a course of instruction from a book or one that has been used elsewhere or before. Adapt teaching appropriately.

We live in days when 'dating' is very common. In some societies now, young people are considered 'strange' if they do not have a boyfriend or girlfriend. This puts pressure on young people to conform and often to behave in ways that are inappropriate to their age. It is a good thing for young people to have a fairly wide circle of friends of both sexes. It is not helpful for them to grow up too restricted in their friendships. Nor, on the other hand, is it good for them to have very little contact with the opposite sex. Unfortunately, in small churches these things can often be the case. Inter-church activities and camps are a great help here. Internet dating is also becoming increasingly common. It is one thing for young people who have already met to keep in contact via the internet. But there are real dangers in developing a 'friendship' with a complete stranger, even if he or she professes to be a Christian.

It needs to be recognised sympathetically that it is possible for those who are still in their early teens to feel very strong attraction to someone of the opposite sex. Rather than forbidding any relationship at all, it is better for this to be kept within the context of a group of friends, if that is possible. Sometimes such an attraction grows and ends in marriage some years later. Often though, it gradually becomes a matter of friendship within the group. It can be part of learning to grow up and this is valuable, provided it does not develop into too close and exclusive a relationship at too young an age.

# 7. Arranged marriage and courtship

This section discusses the way in which two people come to marry. In some cultures marriage is arranged between two families, mainly by parents. The word 'courtship' is old-fashioned but is used here as there is no other suitable alternative. It refers to a developing friendship that leads to marriage after a period of time.

Arranged marriage should be distinguished from forced marriage. The latter takes place when parents insist on a marriage against the will of one of the persons concerned. This is nearly always the woman. The Bible shows us what should happen in Genesis 24. There we read about Abraham's servant who was sent to seek a bride for Isaac. As the story unfolds, it becomes quite clear that Rebekah is to be that bride. God had clearly led the servant to her, 'This is from the LORD' (v.50). Formal approval was given also by her brother and father (v.50–51). Nevertheless, the question was put to Rebekah personally, 'Will you go with this man?' and she replied, 'I will go' (v.58). No-one should be forced to marry against his or her will. Nor should undue pressure ever be put upon a person to consent to a marriage.

Arranged marriages are generally found in societies where generations have lived in the same locality and families know each other well. In these circumstances, parents look for suitable husbands and wives for their children from among families which they know and approve of. These would usually be from the same ethnic, economic and cultural background. Where the custom of arranged marriage has become established, children are normally expected to accept their parents' choice. In many cases this works well. Sometimes the couple already know each other and so can get accustomed to the prospect of marriage. In other circumstances, the couple are expected to be able to make the marriage work and for affection to grow as time goes on. Such marriages are looked upon as perfectly normal in their cultures, and not as a threat to individual choice.

There are both strengths and dangers in arranging marriages. The strength is that families are involved. Both the man and woman themselves set out knowing they must commit themselves to make the marriage work. There are some dangers though. Arranged marriages tend to strengthen divisions in society rather than break them down. This is because such marriages are usually between people belonging to the same cultural group. While couples may often learn to love each other, this does not always happen. Such marriages can then result in great unhappiness. It is also rather easy for the arranging of a marriage to slide towards the enforcing of a marriage. It is necessary to ensure that both the man and woman freely agree to the marriage.

When we look at what took place in Bible times, we can see both arranged marriage and choice by the persons concerned. While Abraham took steps to find a wife for his son Isaac, Isaac and Rebekah's son Esau chose his own wives (Genesis 26:34–35). The other son Jacob was sent to his uncle to find a wife. He fell in love with Rachel, though through trickery he was made to marry her sister first (Genesis 29). The Bible does not insist on either route as the only right way to marriage

In Western countries, marriage most frequently comes at the end of a process of increasing friendship and love. This usually extends over several months at least and may be much longer. In the past, when communities were much closer, the families of the two people, and especially their parents, would naturally take a close interest in any developing relationship. They would often give at least some guidance in the matter. It was the custom for the father of the woman to be asked for and give his permission for marriage to take place. Among richer and more influential families, parents were more often concerned to prevent what was considered an unsuitable marriage. In many wedding services the bride is still given away by her father. This demonstrates the family's approval and joy at the new relationship being entered into.

It is likely that, as time goes by, the way of courtship will become more widespread. This is because people move around more as they seek work. Films and the internet may well encourage this also. Everyone enjoys a love story! Christians, whatever the culture around them, need to consider marriage prayerfully and realistically. It is generally unwise to be too quick in coming to such an important decision. In secular society many young people form relationships with no particular intention of looking towards marriage and these often involve sexual relations. This cannot be the way for Christians. Sex belongs within marriage, not outside of marriage or before it.

More needs to be said on this subject and will be covered positively in the third section of the book.

# 8. A valid marriage

What needs to take place if a couple are to be truly married? What is said here comes from the Bible. It has also found a place in the laws of many countries, though this is beginning to change in some. It must be understood that a valid marriage can take place without necessarily taking place in a church building with an act of worship. Most Christians are likely to desire a marriage in that way, but a civil ceremony is just as valid as a 'Christian' wedding. What actually constitutes a marriage union? The answer can be considered using three headings.

## a. Consent

Both the man and the woman must freely agree to the marriage union taking place. This was established in the last section. In marriage services, consent is usually demonstrated by asking the same sort of question that was asked of Rebekah in Genesis 24. Questions are put to both man and woman which require the answers; 'I do', 'I will'. These answers are given before witnesses, so that there can be no doubt about the willingness of either bride or groom. This also means that there must be a public aspect to the marriage. There are witnesses who can testify to the willingness of both parties to the marriage. The element of consent is very strongly emphasised in the usual marriage services: 'Do you take this woman/man?' 'I do.' 'Will you love her/him?' 'I will.' Those who wish to be married need to be clear about what it is they are doing and give definite consent to the marriage union.

## b. Commitment

This consent also commits each person to the other. So, in a marriage service it is usual for each person to makes promises to the other. These promises have the status of vows. Wherever the ceremony may take place the promises are still made in the presence of God. God is everywhere; he is not found in any one building or place. Each person makes a commitment to be united in love to the other and to be faithful to their commitment in all the varied circumstances of life. Marriage can be called a covenant, or solemn agreement, as the two people have covenanted together (see Malachi 2:14; Proverbs 2:17). This commitment to the other is for the whole of life. It is not a temporary arrangement.

## c. Consummation

According to God's Word, marriage is by definition between a man and a woman. Until very recently, this has also been the general understanding of marriage throughout the world. It is a sexual relationship. Marriage unites the man and woman and that uniting is expressed by becoming 'one flesh' in sexual intercourse. The two persons, having willingly committed themselves to each other, seal that by uniting their bodies. In this way they commence a life lived together. In the past, proof of consummation was required (see Deuteronomy 22:13–21), and still is in some cultures, though rare in these days. Nevertheless it is important to realise that a failure to consummate the marriage means that the marriage has not fully taken place. In most countries the marriage can then legally be declared null and void. Divorce is not possible because there has been no proper marriage. In very rare cases people may go through marriage ceremonies and live celibate lives together, usually on health grounds. For Christians this has to be between them and the Lord. It can be mutually helpful and fulfilling.

# 9. Polygamy

Polygamy means a man has several wives. It occurs quite frequently in the Old Testament and is also still practised among Muslims and in some tribal cultures. It doubtless arose after the flood, as nations lost sight of the creative pattern given by God and followed their own inclinations. There seem to be two particular reasons for the development of polygamy, apart, that is, from lust. It is clear, firstly, that, in Old Testament times, a man's status and strength was demonstrated by marrying a number of wives. It is still the case in some parts of the world. Leaders and kings in particular often had a number of wives. This was also partly due to the fact that alliances with other nations were often sealed by the king marrying someone from the royal family of the country with which the alliance was made (see 1 Kings 3:1).

A second reason may lie in the frequent warfare of those days. This usually resulted in the defeated nation losing large numbers of young men. Even the winners could still experience considerable slaughter. So there would be an excess of women in a population. Polygamy would have seemed a way to compensate for the loss of husbands. Also, if nearly all women of child-bearing age were married, this would help to ensure a good supply of young men in the next generation. Two things are clear. First, this was not God's original plan for marriage. Second, in Old Testament times God tolerated polygamy, even by some of the most well-known of Old Testament saints.

How should we think about polygamy today? Following the teaching of Christ means that we go back to the beginning (Matthew 19:3–7). So Christians will want to marry just one fellow believer in the Lord Jesus. What, however, if someone who already has more than one wife is converted? It has to be remembered that in this case the husband has either explicitly or implicitly made promises to each of his wives. He has responsibilities to them, and also to any children that have been born to him. Unbelievers might have no scruples about divorcing or getting rid of wives, but Christians cannot take that view. Not only would it be wrong to divorce all but the first wife, it would generally leave the divorced wives in a very difficult position. What would happen to them? Would they easily find other husbands? How would they look after themselves in the meanwhile? What about the children; don't they need their father? It is difficult to believe that the right course of action is to break up the family unit. We can see in many societies how harmful the break-up of marriages is, especially to children.

All these considerations indicate that it is better to follow the Old Testament precedent and for the husband to continue to care for all his wives and treat them all equally. An exception would be if a wife herself desired divorce, perhaps because she did not wish to be married to a Christian. It is valuable to look again at Exodus 21:10 concerning a slave wife: 'If he takes another wife to himself, he shall not diminish her food, her clothing, or her marital rights.' A man in this position must seek to avoid favouritism and act fairly and rightly toward each of his wives.

In 1 Timothy 3:2 and 12 it is stated that both elders and deacons must be 'the husband of one wife'. This could be translated as 'a one-woman man'. As Greek culture, in which these instructions were given, was monogamous, this may well refer to men who are faithful in the marriage relationship. It certainly indicates that the leaders in a church are not to be polygamous. This is not just a matter of setting an example of Christian marriage. It also demonstrates that Christian leadership is not a matter of power and prestige, but of service and care for others. A man with more than one wife cannot serve as an elder or deacon.

Polyandry means a woman has more than one husband. This has always been very rare. Group relationships may become legal as some countries change the definition of marriage. Christians must continue to follow the biblical pattern of one man and one woman.

# 10. Birth control and barrenness

Throughout history, most married couples have had quite a number of children. They never even considered any need to restrict the family. Because of the Fall, childbirth has never been easy and child mortality had kept population numbers growing at only a slow rate. The situation in the world now is quite different. Infant mortality in many countries is much reduced and diseases are cured. Many people live well beyond seventy years, especially in developed countries.

The Roman Catholic Church teaches that marriage must be 'open to fertility'. This has been generally understood to mean that no artificial form of birth control is permitted to its members. 'Natural' means of control are permitted; that is, abstinence from sexual intercourse and a method based on the natural rhythms of a woman's menstrual cycle. Protestants also believe that marriages must normally be 'open to fertility'. They do not see, however, that artificial methods of birth control are wrong. In today's world people use spectacles to help them to see, aids to hearing and pacemakers to regulate the heart. It seems inconsistent to prohibit aids to control birth. With these, births can be spaced out and the number restricted. With the world's population growing very rapidly, it is essential for families to be kept smaller than in the past.

The previous paragraph speaks of marriage being 'open to fertility in normal circumstances'. Genesis shows quite clearly that marriage is intended to issue in fruitfulness and the birth of children. There may, however, be circumstances where children are not possible, or where it is not wise for a couple to have any. The most obvious example of such impossibility is when older people marry. No-one, however, would deny the value of the companionship and mutual help which marriage may bring in these cases.

Sometimes a person who gets married may carry some genetic defect or liability to disease, which makes it wise for children not to be born. This has to be a matter of personal decision on medical advice, and between the two persons concerned. In normal circumstances, Christians should not regard marriage as simply a love relationship between two people. Marriage should be open to the possibility of children being born according to the gift of God.

In the case of some couples the problem is not one of controlling birth, but of barrenness. We find this in a number of places in the Bible and its painfulness, especially for a woman, is epitomised by Rachel's bitter cry, 'Give me children, or I shall die!' (Genesis 30:1). Sometimes there is medical or counselling help that can be given, but in the sovereignty of God not every couple is able to have children. Adoption may often be a solution, though this needs to be thought through carefully. Childless people are likely to have many opportunities to be involved in work with children, of course. They—and this includes single people—have often done a great deal for children, both in community and Christian work. They have found this to be fulfilling, and the Lord's will for them, even though it may not be what they would have chosen for themselves.

# 11. Divorce and remarriage

The subject is a difficult one, and Christians do not agree among themselves on exactly how to understand and apply the Bible's teaching on this subject. Living in a fallen world, as we all do, Christians are not immune from the stresses and strains that sometimes occur in marriage. Sadly, in these days, all too many marriages even among Christians come under considerable strain. Divorce is not uncommon, especially in Western countries. So the question of whether remarriage is permissible must also be examined. You will need to think through carefully the view taken here.

As we have seen already, it is quite clear that, though divorce was permitted in the Old Testament, the teaching of Jesus is that marriage is for life: 'What therefore God has joined together, let not man separate' (Matthew 19:6). Christians must understand clearly, before they get married, that God intends marriage to be a lifelong commitment. When things begin to go wrong in a marriage, Christian couples must seek to work things out by prayer and honest discussion together. The church, both by its teaching and readiness to give pastoral guidance and help, should do what it can to enable the couple to sort out their difficulties. However, it is not a straightforward or easy matter.

It needs to be said first of all that ultimately, decisions about divorce and remarriage are the responsibility of those involved. While churches naturally want to obey the Bible and ministers have to preach and teach what they believe to be the truth of God's Word, it is essential to remember some important principles. Firstly, what goes on between a man and his wife is private and personal to them. They may wish for help and guidance if they find themselves in difficulties, and if so they will ask for it. It is inappropriate, though, for ministers to try and intrude into their private life. Marriage guidance and sorting out difficulties is a very sensitive matter.

Secondly, when a couple do come to seek help it is very often after they have already got into considerable difficulty. They may only come as a last resort. It may also be the case that only one of them is really willing to look for help, and the other only agrees to it very reluctantly. In these circumstances it can be too late for anyone to help, and if this is the case it has to be regretfully acknowledged.

Thirdly, the question of pastoral help when a marriage is in difficulty is fraught with dangers. It is important for pastors to gain some proper training and experience before they embark on giving such help themselves. The fact that a pastor may be happily married himself does not guarantee that he can give any useful guidance; it may actually be a hindrance. While a couple will listen to a pastor they respect if he comes alone, in a serious matter this is not generally advisable. It is not at all helpful for two male elders to see a couple who are in trouble; the wife will almost certainly and quite understandably resent this. If the pastor is not married, it is probably best to train up another elder and his wife, or to look for an experienced married pastor from another church.

Fourthly, it is not profitable, and it is an invasion of privacy, for marital problems to be revealed and discussed in church meetings. If, for example, it is public knowledge that adultery has taken place, then this can be recognised and disciplinary action may be taken. Unsubstantiated accusation or supposition cannot be allowed any place in a church meeting. This is an area that needs special care. Church decisions must be based on public facts. Ultimately, all Christians stand and fall to their own Master and Lord, Jesus Christ. Churches are fellowships of love, prayer, service and spiritual guidance, they are not courts of law and members are not jurors. This may seem unsatisfactory to some, but the Lord is the Judge—and we are not to anticipate his verdict.

It is essential to assess divorce in biblical terms: in the Bible it was always the act of one of the partners, not of any official or third party. Nowadays governments have introduced their own laws and these are to be obeyed where they do not directly oppose the Word of God. A Christian understanding of divorce must view it in biblical terms. For example, if a husband simply goes off and abandons his wife, that is biblical divorce, and likewise if a wife does the same. As we have seen, that is what divorce was among Romans in New Testament times and it was similar among the Jews. Usually, of course, such a divorce would be the culmination of disagreements and perhaps unfaithfulness by at least one of the couple.

Making this distinction between biblical divorce and the laws of a country is very important. In the case of a husband abandoning his wife, a Christian wife has often wondered whether it would be right to get a divorce or not. However, in biblical terms, she has already been divorced. When she obtains a state 'divorce' she is only regularising her position in the eyes of the law. In God's eyes, her husband divorced her when he left her. This also helps us when we think of wives who are treated very badly, either physically or psychologically. If a wife is literally driven away by her husband it is right to think of that as equivalent to divorce. No-one can be expected to stay in a situation in which they are exposed to continual violence.

Exodus 21:10–11 is also relevant here: 'If he takes another wife to himself, he shall not diminish her food, her clothing, or her marital rights. And if he does not do these three things for her, she shall go out for nothing, without payment of money.' A slave wife was to be given the full rights of a wife. If these were lacking, her husband was under an obligation to divorce her. This must imply that husbands and wives have mutual obligations which, if they persistently deny these to the other partner, will bring the marriage to an end in divorce. It is, of course, possible for people to abuse both the Bible teaching and state laws on divorce. Marriages do break up that ought not to. Sin is always a possible factor, for real Christians as well as others. The answer, however, is not to adopt an attitude to divorce which cannot be justified by Scripture.

The whole point of divorce is to release the two people from their marriage vows and this makes them eligible to marry again. The divorced are 'unmarried' (1 Corinthians 7:11). If, as we saw when looking at Matthew 5:32, divorce replaces the death penalty laid down in the Old Testament for serious sexual misbehaviour then we can see clearly why this allows for remarriage. The Westminster Confession of Faith (Chapter 24: Of Marriage) says: 'In the case of adultery after marriage, it is lawful for the innocent party to sue out a divorce [i.e. obtain a legal divorce], and, after the divorce, to marry another, as if the offending party were dead.'

It is worth quoting the same Confession again, as it represents the authentic Protestant and Reformation position: 'Although the corruption of man be such as is apt to study arguments, unduly to put asunder those whom God hath joined together in marriage, yet nothing but adultery, or such wilful desertion as can no way be remedied by the church or civil magistrate, is cause sufficient of dissolving the bond of marriage.' 'Wilful desertion', of course, is what takes place when either husband or wife leaves the other and is not willing to return.

'Desertion', however, could also be argued to cover a partner who is prepared to live in the same house, but refuses to live as a married person ought to. This is what we have already seen from Exodus 21:10–11. For example, a married person who unilaterally refuses to engage in sexual union with the other is clearly disobeying Paul's words in 1 Corinthians 7: 'The husband should give to his wife her conjugal rights, and likewise the wife to her husband. For the wife does not have authority over her own body, but the husband does. Likewise the husband does not have authority over his own body, but the wife does. Do not deprive one another, except perhaps by agreement for a limited time, that you may devote yourselves to prayer; but then come together again, so that Satan may not tempt you because of your lack of self-control' (vv.3–5). Clearly and wilfully to desert the responsibilities which people take upon themselves when they marry, will almost certainly lead to divorce. The person who refuses these responsibilities is the one who is to blame for the divorce.

In thinking about divorce it is essential to remember that

circumstances differ and people have different temperaments, strengths and weaknesses. What one person can bear may be intolerable to someone else. For these reasons it is seriously mistaken to try and lay down anything more than general guidelines for helping people with marriage difficulties. Pastoral care is an art which is developed through experience, as Bible precepts and principles are wisely applied to individual cases.

# 12. Girls, women and widows

It is a sad and tragic fact that in many parts of the world girls are still valued only as suitable marriage partners. In addition many girls are abused sexually (and in other ways), often from quite a young age. Girls—and boys—are to be valued most of all because they are human beings. They are made in the image of God, made to serve and glorify him. Most boys and girls will get married, and that is in the purpose of God too. However, neither must be valued merely as marriage partners. They are persons in their own right who can have fruitful and useful lives to God's glory, whether or not they get married. These truths must shape the thinking and attitudes of Christians.

Tragically, sexual abuse of girls is very widespread, and Christians need to realise that this is so and stand against it. It may be asking too much for every church to have some woman with training and skill in helping other women overcome the effects of abuse, but experience shows there is a widespread need. Some difficulties in marriage can often be traced back to such abuse. The sexualisation of young girls by Western media, and the opportunity for young children to view pornography, is already having serious consequences. Sex education in schools at a very early age is almost certainly adding to the problem rather than helping to solve it.

It is becoming increasingly difficult for children from Christian homes who attend any schools other than those that are explicitly Christian. This is not just because the explicit sex education they will receive is taken out of the context of creation which it has in the Bible. In addition, the attitudes, behaviour and jokes of other children will make them stand out unless they conform. They need the prayers of God's people, and supported by prayer, their parents need real wisdom in order to guide and help them. Yet there is wisdom in the Bible and grace from our heavenly Father for every need and situation.

In many parts of the world, women are still too frequently treated as second class people. It is not too difficult to see how this will have come about. In the past it was obvious that, in most cases, the husband would be the breadwinner while the wife would bear children and care for them in their early years. As boys grew up, they would accompany their fathers and learn skills from him. Girls would remain in the home and learn to help in the domestic tasks which women carried out around the house.

It would have been easy for men with skill in hunting or warfare to look down upon stay at home women, looking after little children. Sadly, sometimes women were treated as not much more than baby producers, subjected to pregnancy after pregnancy. The fact is, however, that the woman's task of caring for the next generation was every bit as important as the man's role. Times may have changed since then, but bad attitudes die hard. Sin affects relationships and Christians must learn from

Scripture, and not from cultures that demean women. It would also be wrong to think of life in terms of a battle between men and women. We need one another and must learn to work together with each other.

Now that parents have reason to be careful about the number of children they have, women who get married have greater opportunities for work and careers outside the home. We need to be balanced in our thinking. Caring for children in the early years is a vital task, and only when circumstances make it necessary should this be compromised by seeking other employment. However, some women do not marry, and not all of those who do marry may be able to have children. Such women should use their God-given abilities to the fullest possible extent, as the Lord enables. The same applies, of course, to mothers once their children are at school.

Christian women will often want to use their gifts in Christian or community work if there are opportunities for this. So far as church work is concerned, there are many areas in which women can be engaged, though usually this will be voluntary and unpaid. Some understand 1 Timothy 3:11 to teach that women can be deacons (the word 'wives' could also be translated 'women'; see also Romans 16:1). Many women are found in the pages of the New Testament, some of whom were very faithful believers and a great example of love for Jesus Christ. It is true that the twelve apostles were all men and the instructions for pastors—that is, teachers, overseers, elders—indicate that only men are to be chosen for this service (1 Timothy 3:1–7; Titus 1:5–9). Women are explicitly excluded from the public teaching and preaching ministry of the church (1 Corinthians 14:33–37; 1 Timothy 2:11–15). This, of course, does not exclude them from many other opportunities to teach and give guidance within the local church and beyond.

None of this implies that women are of lesser importance or of lesser status than men. It is simply that God has called them to different roles in the church, as also in the home. In fact all ministry in the church is servant ministry, no-one has any higher status than any other. Ministry is not a symbol or expression of power; it is an opportunity to serve others for Christ's sake. No man has any authority over others in himself. Authority derives only from the Word of God which is preached and which all can read, understand and obey for themselves. Moreover, it is a solemn thing to be a teacher in the church: 'Not many of you should become teachers, my brothers, for you know that we who teach will be judged with greater strictness' (James 3:1).

Just as girls and women are often treated very badly in many countries, widows are also terribly abused in some parts of the world. This is in stark contrast to what the Bible teaches. In the Old Testament, God specifically declares that he cares for widows. He ensured specific provision was made for them in Israel, along with orphans and immigrants: 'For the LORD your God is God of gods and Lord of lords, the great, the mighty, and the awesome God, who is not partial and takes no bribe. He executes justice for the fatherless and the widow, and loves the sojourner, giving him food and clothing' (Deuteronomy 10:17–18; see also, for example, 14:28–29; 16:9–11).

In the New Testament we have the example of the Lord Jesus, who, even as he was suffering untold agonies on the cross, ensured that his mother, Mary, would be provided for after his death and resurrection: 'When Jesus saw his mother and the disciple whom he loved standing nearby, he said to his mother, "Woman, behold, your son!" Then he said to the disciple, "Behold, your mother!" And from that hour the disciple took her to his own home' (John 19:26–27).

We also find that the early church in Jerusalem first expressed its care for those in need by providing for the widows (Acts 6:1–7). Paul says that he thinks it is good for widows to remain unmarried, but makes it quite clear that they can be married in the Lord if they wish (1 Corinthians 7:8–9, 39–40). He was obviously concerned for widows, and also realised the way in which they could be very useful in the church. In 1 Timothy 5:3–16 he spends some time dealing with this matter.

He is very clear that the first responsibility for care belongs to the family, the children or grandchildren of the widow (vv.4–8). However, it is also the case that some widows who were experienced and godly believers were being provided for by the church. Paul gives guidance about this. Those with a good reputation, who were at least sixty, could be put on a list. It seems that they would also fulfil a teaching and helping role among younger women (see also Titus 2:3–5). His opening words in 1 Timothy 5:3 set the agenda for Christians: 'Honour widows who are truly widows'. How different from the neglect so often found in the world!

# 13. Homosexuality

It is necessary to consider this because of the days in which we live. In a number of countries, it is now possible for a man to marry a man, or a woman to marry a woman. There is pressure for the law to be changed in many other countries too. In some societies, it has been the custom for this to take place on occasion, though it has not been specified in any law. The Bible is very clear that from the very beginning marriage is between a man and a woman. Man and woman were created by God to fit together physically. Marriage, and the sexual relationship which it involves, can only be entered by a man and a woman, not by two people of the same sex.

The Bible goes further than this, however. It teaches that sexual intercourse should not take place between people of the same sex. It does so by highlighting bad examples and by explicit prohibitions (see Genesis 19:4–22; Leviticus 18:22; 20:13; Judges 19; Romans 1:24–28; 1 Corinthians 6:9–11; 1 Timothy 1:8–11; Jude 7). It is clear that God sees such behaviour as a serious deviation from the created pattern. Paul's words in the passage from 1 Corinthians are very weighty: 'Do you not know that the unrighteous will not inherit the kingdom of God? Do not be deceived: neither the sexually immoral, nor idolaters, nor adulterers, nor men who practice homosexuality, nor thieves, nor the greedy, nor drunkards, nor revilers, nor swindlers will inherit the kingdom of God.'

We should note from the passage above that it is homosexual activity which is spoken about, and that this is included as one in a list of other sins. In fact, it is in the same list as those who are greedy! Serious though such behaviour is, we should not isolate it as if it is in a category all on its own. There are also other sexual sins listed. Sexual behaviour is an area where there have always been many temptations, but this is even more the case today, with explicit films and pornography on the internet. Christians are called to keep themselves pure, and to restrict sexual intercourse to the marriage relationship alone.

Just as today consensual sex outside of marriage is considered perfectly acceptable in many countries, so also are homosexual relations. Even some countries that do not allow for homosexual marriage may have some form of civil partnership which gives to homosexual couples equal rights with those who are married. Some homosexual couples do enter into long-term relationships, and governments believe it right to recognise such relationships and grant appropriate legal rights. While Christians cannot approve of these relationships, we recognise that people are free to disobey the commands of God. Freedom of religion also means that governments allow people the right to their own beliefs and practices, but do not legislate in favour of any one religion. However, while this sounds fine in theory, it is much more difficult in practice. It is, nonetheless, what Western style democratic governments at least aim for.

In many parts of the world, homosexual people have often been treated extremely badly. They have suffered ostracism, ridicule, rejection and violence. This may have been the case even when they did not actually engage in any sexual activity. Christians cannot justify such attitudes or behaviour and must not themselves be guilty of these. We are all sinners and only God is able to see our hearts and come to a right judgement of our guilt. Jesus came down hard on the pride and arrogance of self-righteous, outwardly religious, people. He also met and welcomed prostitutes, and Jews who worked for the Romans as tax-collectors. The good news of Jesus Christ is only for sinners— and it calls out to the most depraved and the most hardened.

The words 'homosexual' and 'gay' are used frequently these days. We need to understand that they are broad terms. Some described in this way have only ever felt a sexual attraction to those of their own sex. Others are described as 'bisexual'; that is, they can be attracted to either sex. While some have been helped to enter into a normal marriage, this is not the case with others. There are also other forms of sexual deviance, which we cannot consider here. The plain truth is that God has given us marriage and, apart from marriage, human beings are to live celibate lives. Many Christians down through the centuries have remained single and been much used by God for his glory. This can still be the same today. It is not easy for Christians who feel an attraction to those of the same sex. They need understanding and loving support from those believers with whom they share their situation.

Homosexuals are as much in need of the gospel as any others. It is our responsibility to make the gospel known to all men and women, and it should be done with compassion and understanding. We have to be very careful to ensure that our attitude is not to condemn homosexuals—it is God who condemns sinners when the time comes. We must be concerned to win them for Jesus Christ. This is not easy. Many are prejudiced against Christianity, often because they believe Christians are prejudiced against them. Our duty is not to impose Christian standards of morality on society, but to seek to change lives through the gospel.

# 14. Law, custom and wisdom

We have already seen that the laws of a country may differ from what the Bible teaches. Christians are obligated to obey the law unless the law commands them to disobey God. In these circumstances, they must be prepared to submit to the law by suffering the penalties which it imposes. The law is upheld both by obedience to it and by receiving its penalties. Suffering the penalty of the law may possibly become the case when it comes to marriage, when the law is changed to admit the 'marriage' of homosexuals. In other circumstances where Christian marriage may differ from a country's law, Christians should see that they also fulfil the law's requirements.

In some countries, there are long-standing customs regarding marriage. If these do not conflict with Christian teaching, it is wise to follow custom as far as this is possible. This is the case, for example, with arranged marriages. Provided young people are not forced against their will, marriages arranged by the families concerned are perfectly acceptable. Moreover, in Western countries it is better if engagements take place with the full knowledge and approval of the families concerned. Not all customs, however, are beneficial. There may be cases where churches have to take a stand against an established custom. For example, a pastor should not be prepared to take a polygamous marriage. At least, not in normal circumstances (see below).

Pastors and churches also have, at times, to exercise wisdom and accept what is best in the circumstances. Let us suppose that an unmarried couple live together and have several children. One of the partners is converted to Jesus Christ and naturally ought to belong to the church which he or she attends. As the couple are not married, the right thing to do would be to regularise their condition formally by marriage. The unconverted partner, however, may see no reason to get married after so many years together. In these circumstances it would be wrong to say that the converted partner should leave the other partner and the children. Wisdom says that they are living as if married; they have stayed together for years, they are bringing up a family. There is no point in causing an upset or division between the man and the woman (the conversion itself may have already caused some tension). It is best to accept the situation as it is, and allow the Christian to join the church.

The Bible gives no guidance at all on any essential marriage ceremony. So the view could be taken that the couple in the case mentioned are already tacitly married. Up until the 1950s, for example, it was possible to be married in Scotland 'by repute and custom'. Something similar may still obtain in other parts of the world.

Let us return briefly to polygamy. Suppose a man was living with several women, perhaps with children by all of them. He is converted and decides that he ought to be married. It may also be that this will mean that they will share his inheritance when he dies. In those circumstances it is not necessary for a church to oppose a polygamous marriage. A pastor may believe it could only do good, in these circumstances, for him to take a part, even if only to preach a message.

When West Indians began to come to Britain after the Second World War, a difficulty arose because of a marriage custom on the part at of least some of them. A wedding ceremony with a celebration following were very important to them, but a couple often could not afford anything that seemed appropriate. So, they would live together and children might be born. Then, when they had saved enough money, they would have a grand wedding to which all the family would be invited. Sometimes their own children might be bridesmaids. How should this be viewed? That there were dangers in this practice is obvious, but in numbers of cases it was quite clear that the couple were completely committed to each other.

It is undeniable that many Christians will feel disquiet over situations like these described. The fact remains, though, that irregular situations do sometimes arise. They are also likely to arise more often, as people are increasingly secularised. Paul, in 1 Corinthians 10:27, writes of a situation where he says believers can eat meat 'without raising any question on the ground of conscience'. There are other situations like that. There are also situations that have no obvious answer. A married minister in the British parliament once promised his lover that he would divorce his wife and marry her. As a result they had a child together. However, he then changed his mind and stayed with his wife. His sin had brought about a situation where whatever he did was wrong. Who would want to have to counsel someone in that position?

Ministers and churches must realise that the law of the land is not in their hands. They have no right to interfere in the private lives of people. Unless there are reasons for doubt, they have to accept what people say and take them on trust. They must avoid a legalistic approach and accept those who give every appearance of true repentance. This may seem risky, but everything must be done with prayer and committing all things into the hands of God. God promises wisdom to those who ask for it (James 1:5–8; 3:13–18).

# Part 3: Christian Marriage

# 15. Introduction

This section seeks to give positive guidance and help. There are some things that the Bible says about marriage that all Christians must accept and live by. There is also biblical advice which depends on circumstance. For example in 1 Peter 3:1–3 there is both principle and advice for converted wives who live with unconverted husbands. They are to be submissive to their husbands; that is a Bible principle. The way they are to win their husbands to Christ, however, is by their attitude and conduct rather than by the Word. That is advice for those in that situation. This section will give general advice, but there may be some circumstances in which it is not the best advice to follow. There can sometimes be exceptions to what is the usual rule.

Part of the reason for making this point at the beginning is that we are all different. We live in different cultures and the Christian life is not simply following a set of rules. There are, of course, laws in the Bible, but there are also teachings and principles which can be applied in various ways. More than that; God has given us minds so that we can think through how we ought to live. For example, it is generally wise for two people who are beginning to feel mutually attracted to take their time. It is not usually sensible to rush into a relationship with hopes that it will lead to marriage. However, if they are only going to be in each other's company for short periods of time, then it would be a good idea to correspond with each other when they are parted. In addition, temperament also enters into this. Some people take their time and may even be rather slow. Others are just the opposite.

It is important to understand this. Christians often face two wrong alternatives; that of making up their own laws, or adopting a rather careless attitude to life. Some approach the Bible in an unthinking way, and make rules for life which cannot be justified from what the Bible says. Others are slack when it comes to obeying clear commands in Scripture. Growth in grace and understanding leads to a life that joyfully keeps God's commands. Wise Christians do not bind themselves or others to a thoughtless lifestyle. They take differing circumstances and needs into account. Pastors and those who teach and guide in churches need to remember all this too.

# 16. Before marriage

As young people grow through their teenage years and begin to enter their twenties, they will naturally be thinking about the possibility of marriage. If they are wise Christians, they will be praying about their future. They will ask God to lead them in every area of their life. They will also read the Bible regularly. In this way they will get to know what it has to say about the will of God and the many different ways in which Christians can serve him. Unless there are exceptional circumstances, they should also be members of a church. They will regularly worship God and listen to the explanation of God's Word.

These things are very important. Some may not be able to have the church fellowship that they would like. Others may be brought up in a home that is unsympathetic to the gospel. If so, they need to do what they can by reading the Bible, praying and asking for God's clear guidance. At the same time, young Christians need to realise that God generally guides us as we use our minds. We should apply what the Bible says to ourselves. We should seek to understand what our own gifts and abilities are. We should look out to see what opportunities there may be, whether for training or employment. God often guides us through circumstances. In his providence, he leads us to gain certain knowledge or skills which he wants us to use.

We have to understand that it is not the will of God for every Christian to be married. Those who do get married may not do so in their early twenties. For some, a significant number of years may pass before marriage. This reminds us that we must be looking to serve God as we are. Single people have many different roles that they can perform for Christ. These may be in what we call secular employment as well as in more specific Christian service. Most Christians serve God and their communities in normal avenues of employment. These are just as much a calling from God as any other. The Bible tells us we should do everything for the glory of God (1 Corinthians 10:31). It tells servants to serve those over them as 'servants of Christ', 'with a good will as to the Lord and not to man' (Ephesians 6:6,7).

Remember, too, that marriage, while it brings many blessings, also brings stresses and strains. The apostle Paul said: 'I want you to be free from anxieties. The unmarried man is anxious about the things of the Lord, how to please the Lord. But the married man is anxious about worldly things, how to please his wife, and his interests are divided. And the unmarried or betrothed woman is anxious about the things of the Lord, how to be holy in body and spirit. But the married woman is anxious about worldly things, how to please her husband. I say this for your own benefit, not to lay any restraint upon you, but to promote good order and to secure your undivided devotion to the Lord' (1 Corinthians 7:32–35). It is often the case in Western countries that there are more young women in churches than young men and this means more single women Christians. Every believer is loved by Jesus Christ and can serve him, whether married or not.

Nevertheless, most Christians do get married and it is right to pray and prepare for the possibility. So it is important to understand what the Bible says about marriage—that is why this book has been written. It is also important to have a factual understanding of sexuality and sexual relations. In these days sex education is more and more taught in schools. However, the teaching in many schools needs to be considered and understood in the light of what the Bible has to say.

Sometimes a person may have to make a very difficult decision, if there is an attraction towards someone who is an unbeliever. Some Christians have been enabled to bring another to faith in Jesus Christ, whom they have then gone on to marry, but this by no means always happens. Exact circumstances need to be taken into account and they may differ considerably in different countries. As a general rule believers should marry believers.

Young people can very often act unwisely. Nowadays young people in many countries start having boyfriends or girlfriends at an early age. In many cases these relationships involve sexual behaviour, all too often leading up to full intercourse. It is not unusual for a young person to have several such friendships over the years. Too many who are converted later on look back and wish they had behaved differently. It is true that we can learn by hard experience, but some experiences are best avoided. It is not a good preparation for marriage, when it comes, to have to look back with sorrow over one's behaviour with previous boy or girl friends. Christian young people must obey the Scriptures, avoid putting themselves into situations of temptation, and keep themselves pure.

# 17. Towards marriage

In the Western world when people think of marriage, they have in mind two people 'falling in love', as the saying goes. Right from almost the first meeting, some feel drawn to each other, sometimes very powerfully. This, though, is nothing like as usual as romantically inclined people think. Sometimes, it is only one person who falls in love, but the other does not, though he or she may do so in time. More often, love is a gradual thing as two people get to know each other and find they have interests in common. There is no point in anyone expecting or hoping that love will come in any particular way. Two people may meet when they are in the company of others as, for example, at a young peoples' group at church. It is not wise for them to pair up very quickly and begin an exclusive relationship. Rather, to continue to meet within a group is useful. It is actually easier to get to know more about a person in those circumstances, than when a couple become absorbed in each other.

It is a good thing to begin with friendship and let the relationship deepen naturally as it takes its course. Obviously, two people will want to find out about each other in conversation, but that needs to be gradual and natural. It is unwise to try to find out too much at the beginning and to cross-question the other too much. In time, Christians should want to speak about spiritual things. It is important to talk about how each one came to know the Lord and the development of their spiritual life. As time goes on, conversation will turn to those things which are very important for each of them. There is the possibility of disagreement, and perhaps a need for them to modify some belief or understanding which has been taken for granted without thinking through.

It is perfectly possible for people who differ in a number of ways and who have a very different outlook on some matters to be happily married. But some things are more important, and may cause real problems if they are not sorted out. These include matters such as how to bring up children, what sort of schooling they should have, and what church to belong to. Watch out for issues which seem likely to cause real disagreements. Temperament also comes into this. Some people can easily live together and agree to disagree, others cannot! It is important for people to be honest with themselves. It is not a good thing to shut one's eyes to possible incompatibilities—marriage is a lifelong commitment. There is a saying that those who marry in haste may have to repent at leisure. It is a good one to keep in mind.

During an important stage of life like this, Christians will naturally be much in prayer that they will do what is right before God. They do not need any special signs from God; love for the other is itself an indication of his will. Love is more than sexual attraction, though it does include it. While it is true that love grows and develops, to marry without love in a culture that knows nothing of arranged marriage is a mistake. Two Christians may share much in common, but for marriage they need to love each other.

# 18. Engagement

It is still the custom in many countries for the man to 'propose' to the woman, that is, to ask her to marry him. When she accepts they become engaged; that is, committed to marry each other. It is also the custom in some countries for the man to ask the woman's father for permission to marry her. This is a good practice, because it means the family is involved. Marriage not only links two people, but two families as well—at least to some extent. Engagement is usually sealed and publicly demonstrated by giving a ring to the woman.

Engagement is very similar to the custom of betrothal which we read about in the Bible. However, that form of betrothal could only be broken by divorce (cf. Matthew 1:18–19), whereas this is no longer the case with engagement in Western countries. In the past, if a man broke off an engagement, in some countries he could be sued in the courts by the woman for 'breach of promise', but that is no longer the case. When an engagement is called off it may well cause great heartache, especially if it is a one-sided decision. However, it is better to have a broken engagement than a miserable or broken marriage. Better still is only to get engaged when both man and woman are sure of each other.

Christians have their own times of personal and private Bible reading and prayer. This practice will need to continue within marriage. Sometimes, Christians begin to pray together as they get to know each other better. It is wiser, however, to wait for this until they are engaged, because until that point there is no commitment to each other. Once they are committed, they can then plan together prayerfully, seeking to live as God tells us in the Bible.

Circumstances differ, but it is best for an engagement not to last too long. This is especially so if the couple are regularly in each other's company. Being in love and committed to marriage, but waiting a long time before the marriage can be consummated, puts sexual pressure on both of them. There are many things to think about and to get settled. Where are they going to live? Can they both continue to work? What about children: when will they hope to start a family, how many will they desire to have? How will they handle money; should they have a joint bank account or separate ones? If one or both are going to move away from where they have lived, what church will they belong to?

The answers to these questions, and others like them, will depend partly upon circumstances and also the culture in which the couple live. The important thing, though, is that they are all prayed about and discussed honestly together. Often the first big test of their relationship will come as they get down to practicalities like this. There will generally have to be a measure of give and take. At the same time, it is important to realise that some of their plans or intentions may have to be altered because of circumstances they have not foreseen.

In these days, young couples seem to like to start, if they can, with a house, new furniture and a car. Often large sums of money are spent on the wedding itself. Christians need to ask themselves whether all this can be justified. They must realise that we are stewards of the money that the Lord has enabled us to earn. This perspective needs to be in place at the very beginning of their life together. More will be said of the wedding in a moment, but there is a general principle here. God needs to be honoured in a marriage right from the start. Questions like, 'would it be right to start married life with debt?' Or, 'are we showing off or even trying to outdo others?' need to be honestly faced. Money matters need to be thought through and prayed over, as the couple prepare to live their lives together.

Yet this is an exciting and joyful time. Wise and thoughtful preparation should not be allowed to dampen the sense of anticipation. True love between a man and a woman is a wonderful thing; it is a great gift of a good God. Marriage will have its challenges, its stresses and strains at times. Life in a fallen world is like that. But marriage is a great blessing from God, and should be looked forward to with thankful anticipation. 'Two are better than one, because they have a good reward for their toil. For if they fall, one will lift up his fellow' (Ecclesiastes 4:9–10). 'Many waters cannot quench love, neither can floods drown it' (Song of Solomon 8:7).

# 19. The wedding

The precise form in which two people are married generally depends on the custom in their culture. The first wedding the Bible tells us about is that between Jacob and Leah—though it should have been between Jacob and Rachel. 'Then Jacob said to Laban, "Give me my wife that I may go in to her, for my time is completed." So Laban gathered together all the people of the place and made a feast. But in the evening he took his daughter Leah and brought her to Jacob, and he went in to her' (Genesis 29:21–23). We can see that this was a public event; all the people in the place were invited. It was also a time of celebration, there was a feast. These two characteristics seem to recur throughout the Bible when it speaks of weddings.

Jesus was called, with his disciples, to a wedding in Cana of Galilee (John 2:1–11). It was probably the marriage of a relative of his from what is said of Mary, his mother. Once again there was feasting, and in those days this could go on for several days—though only after work in the evening. Not only does the presence of Jesus at the wedding show that God's blessing rests

on such an event, Jesus also spoke of weddings in his parables
(Matthew 22:1–14; 25:1–13). Strikingly, the joy of heaven is pictured
as a marriage supper (Revelation 19:6–10).

So from the Bible we learn that a wedding—the joining of a
man and woman in marriage—is an occasion of joy when relatives
and friends are invited. There was feasting before the bride and
groom went to spend their first night together. There was also
'the friend of the bridegroom', who is roughly the equivalent of
what we now call the best man. The parable of the ten virgins
shows that there were young women who accompanied the bride,
the equivalent of today's bridesmaids. We noted earlier that the
Bible says nothing about any religious service of marriage. It
is certainly very appropriate for two believers to be united in
marriage in a service of the worship of God. We might add that
in some countries the newly married couple will often go away
for a holiday—the honeymoon.

A wedding is clearly a very important day in the lives of those
being married. Best clothes—usually new—are worn for the
occasion. The bride especially tries to have a dress befitting the
occasion, with special dresses for the bridesmaids also. While
these things are not essential, it is right to make the ceremony
a special one. Clothes, guests, a public service, a special meal
together—all these things combine to set such an occasion
apart. To have a wedding service using memorable and suitable
words and passages of Scripture, appropriate hymns and prayers,
completes the occasion.

There are traditional forms for wedding services in English,
and doubtless in other languages too. Here it is enough to suggest
that there should be appropriate questions and promises. It is
usual for the bride to be given away by her father, or in cases
where this is not possible, a suitable male relative. This parallels

the way that God brought Eve to Adam (Genesis 2:22). There will usually be an address from the Bible. Sometimes this is directed especially to the couple, giving biblical counsel for a married life. Often Christians wish for this to be evangelistic, so that relatives and friends may hear the gospel. It is important not to underestimate the witness of a Christian wedding, even if there is no direct explanation of the gospel.

In Deuteronomy 24:5 there is a remarkable provision which God gave to Israel: 'When a man is newly married, he shall not go out with the army or be liable for any other public duty. He shall be free at home one year to be happy with his wife whom he has taken.' While we should not understand this to be intended for today or practical in today's circumstances, it does set before us an important truth. In the early days a husband and wife need to spend time getting to know each other in a deeper way and adjusting to a coupled life rather than a single one.

The honeymoon, the holiday which the newly married couple usually take together immediately after the wedding, is the beginning of this process. This may not take place in every culture, nor be possible in every circumstance. It does give the couple space and time to express their love to each other and recover from all the pressures which are usual in the build-up to a marriage. They should treat each other with tenderness and thoughtfulness. This is the time when sexual intercourse begins. They need to adjust to each other and learn how to please each other and relax together in each other's company.

The early months of married life are important too. As far as possible, couples should free themselves from too many other responsibilities, so that they can get their home together and cement the relationship that has begun. This is not simply a matter of looking inward to their own relationship. It is also to enable them to look outward together in service, church life and Christian witness. They are now yoked together and have to learn how to serve in tandem. This may not be so easy if they have both had several years of very active and fulfilled lives as single people. Learning together and working together take time but bring their own rewards.

# 20. Husbands and wives

At this point we need to turn back to Ephesians 5:22–33 (see also Colossians 3:18–19; 1 Peter 3:1–7). It is essential to start with the analogy which Paul brings before us, the relationship between Christ and his church. Everything depends on seeing marriage in the light of this example. Christ loves the church, he cherishes it; he is always actively working for the real good of the church. He sacrificed himself for the church and his great concern is for the church to be perfect, holy and without blemish. And it will be one day, the day of the great marriage supper of the Lamb (Revelation 19:6–9).

In marriage, husband and wife are both to live according to the pattern of that relationship. They are to see how the specific instructions Paul gives to each work out in the light of Christ and his church. Moreover, neither husband nor wife is to think of their own roles in the light of what is said to the other. The husband is not to deduce from the fact that wives are told to submit to their husbands that he can order her around! The wife is not to deduce from the fact that her husband is told to love her that he should give her and do for her whatever she asks! Both are to consider their own responsibilities in the light of the relationship between Christ and the church.

It must be remembered that the analogy does not apply in every respect. Jesus Christ is God as well as man; he is perfect in all his thoughts and actions. A husband is just a man, even at his best. He is a sinner even if he has been saved by grace and is making some progress in holiness. His wife will not need to be told these things! He must not think of himself more highly than he ought. Neither husband nor wife is perfect and they cannot expect perfection in their marriage. They must work together to make their relationship the very best that it can be, seeking to grow together in love and holiness.

Although the wife is addressed first there is much more said to the husband than to the wife. Clearly, if 'the husband is the head of the wife' then more in the relationship depends on him and his behaviour than on the wife. If one's head is thinking properly, then what the body does will be appropriate and beneficial. For this reason we will begin with the husband, though it will not be possible in a short space to trace out all that the apostle teaches in this passage.

The first, and probably the most important point is this: the couple have now become 'one flesh' (v.31). Just as the union between Christ and his church is a profound mystery, so also is the union between a man and a woman in marriage. Prior to marriage, in normal circumstances, the closest human relationship for the man is with his mother and father. They are flesh and blood relatives, there is a tie between them of a nature that there cannot be with anyone else. But that tie gives way to one that is even deeper: the union of a man and woman in marriage. That union is brought about and symbolised in sexual intercourse, but it is also a growing and developing unity of mind, heart and purpose. The remarkable thing is that husband and wife can be very different in many ways as individuals and yet become wonderfully united in their life together.

This union exists but it also needs to be protected, promoted and developed. The husband therefore needs 'to love his wife as himself' (v.33). 'In the same way husbands should love their wives as their own bodies. He who loves his wife loves himself. For no one ever hated his own flesh, but nourishes it and cherishes it, just as Christ does the church' (vv.28–29). Once a man really grasps this truth, he begins to understand what his role in marriage is. Just as Christ's love for the church was expressed by self-sacrifice, so must the love of the husband for the wife be. Just as Christ's love for the church is an ongoing, long term love, so also the husband is called to the same sort of love. Just as Christ's love for the church is not a love from the outside, trying to change and alter those who are not in union with him, so also in marriage. The husband is not like a teacher or carer helping someone else. Husband and wife belong together and, as Christians, Christ's love unites them and deepens their relationship more and more.

This love is to be reciprocated by the wife. Her submission means that she understands how her husband is seeking to deepen the relationship and she joins in this, receiving his love and responding to it. It is a joint venture with the husband taking the lead. Yet we must never forget that husband and wife are equal; each will have their own particular gifts and abilities. A wife might be cleverer than her husband or much more practically minded, but this does not have any bearing on her responsive submissiveness. The teaching here is not about gifts or even necessarily actions, it is about the mutuality of love. Love should influence and sweeten every aspect of their lives together.

In practical terms, there will be many things that husband and wife will need to talk over and many decisions to make. Some will be about important matters, others less so. Usually it will be possible to come to agreement about what action to take, whether it be buying a house or moving a piece of furniture. In reaching decisions, there will be occasions when the husband recognizes that his wife's suggestions are better than his own. Even when he would prefer his own idea, he will often defer to his wife. After all, he loves her and wants her to be satisfied.

There may, however, come occasions when an important decision has to be taken and neither of them is quite sure of the best course of action. There might even be a complete disagreement between them. In these circumstances, the husband's place is to take the decision. He may believe it to be wiser to give way to his wife, but even then the final decision is his, for which he takes the responsibility. He does what he believes is in the best interests of both of them, and of any family which they have. His wife is to accept this, and if his decision proves not to be the best, she should avoid the temptation to say, 'I told you so!' He was acting, in a difficult situation, in what he believed was best for them both. Any such discussions and decisions should take place with prayer and in a spirit of understanding love.

This passage completely prohibits any form of physical or verbal violence being used by a husband to his wife—and, of course, by the wife to her husband. Violence against wives is far too common in many countries. Even Christians have been known to lose their temper and act utterly out of character. It is more likely with Christians that their words should be watched. It is possible to belittle the other, to use sarcasm, to react or reply with an ungodly attitude. None of us is perfect, and it is all too easy to say the harsh word and so hard to say, 'Sorry'. There will always be some occasions when one must apologise to the other, and it should be done wholeheartedly and without reserve.

1 Peter 3:1–7 adds to the picture we are given in Ephesians and several points need to be noticed. Firstly, Peter uses a beautiful phrase about a Christian couple. They are 'heirs together of the grace of life' (v.7, AV). What is 'the grace of life'? Perhaps it could be understood in more than one way, but the following seems the most obvious. Their life together as a married couple is a free gift; it comes from God as a gift of his grace. It is not simply that they have decided to get married; in the purpose of God they belong together. The life that stretches before them—even with its ups and downs, its challenges and disappointments—is the wonderful gift of their heavenly Father. They can go forward in it with confidence. They can enjoy together all the blessings that it brings.

In the opening verses of the passage, Peter addresses wives and he has those married to unbelievers particularly in mind. Nevertheless, most of what he says applies to all married women. His focus is on the life and the heart, on behaviour and attitude: 'respectful and pure conduct', 'the imperishable beauty of a gentle and quiet spirit, which in God's sight is very precious'. Those last words are very important. However unappreciative some husbands may be—and many fail at this point—God sees the heart and values what is precious to him.

Peter also warns against a common mistake: 'Do not let your adorning be external—the braiding of hair, the wearing of gold, or the putting on of clothing.' Clearly he is not saying that women should not be suitably dressed, it is the priority and the contrast which is important. The person is more important than what she wears. Outward beauty can simply be a cover for inward ugliness. There is also a suggestion of unnecessary extravagance here: wearing gold, having an expensive hairstyle.

When he turns to husbands, Peter tells them that they should 'live with your wives in an understanding way'. Many husbands jokingly profess that they have never understood their wives, but if that is really so, it is a sin. Of course we never understand another person fully and perfectly ('For who knows a person's thoughts except the spirit of that person, which is in him [or her]?' 1 Corinthians 2:11). However, part of growing together in marriage is that there is an increasing understanding of the other's personality, temperament, strengths and weaknesses. When Peter speaks of the woman as 'the weaker vessel' he is probably commenting on the usual disparity of physical strength, though women can also be more sensitive, and feel things more deeply, than men do. Husbands are to take Peter's words to heart.

The final point is very important. Ignorance and an uncaring, thoughtless attitude will hinder the prayers of the couple. Unless husband and wife are both seeking by God's grace to obey what he has said to them in Scripture, their praying will be affected. What value is it to pray for God's blessing on your marriage, if you don't pay attention to what God has said about married life? Can prayer make up for carelessness or disobedience?

A little later we shall consider the stresses and strains which are inevitable in married life in the world as it is, but these must be mentioned here also. Otherwise, what we have considered may seem a counsel of perfection that is completely unattainable. There will be illnesses, sometimes serious or long-term, which will have to be negotiated, and priorities may have to change. Certain inadequacies on both sides will become evident which will have to be understood and allowed for. There will be mistakes and sins. There will need to be repentance and apology. There will be foolish behaviour, unwise decisions and failure to learn by experience. But through all these, there is grace from God. Grace for new beginnings and for real progress in love, understanding and mutual care.

# 21. A Christian home

Married Christians will want to establish what we can call a Christian home. There is, of course, no blueprint for this in the Bible and there is no intention of trying to set out one here. Certain things will be true, but there may be considerable differences in the way this works out in individual cases. People have different employments and different responsibilities, so the way their lives are ordered will be different. Some men have to leave home early in the morning; nursing mothers may have to feed a baby several times during a night. Things change as time goes by, so there will be alteration in the way a family's time is ordered.

All Christians need to read the Bible regularly and to pray, so these will have to be fitted into the routine of the home. It is important for both husband and wife to have their own personal times of devotion, but they need also to have such a time together. In the early days after marriage this may be straightforward and it is good to get a pattern established. For example, each may seek the Lord separately in the morning and then together at

the end of the day. It could, of course, be the other way round.
Jesus Christ gave thanks before meals (John 6:11; Luke 22:19)
and this is a good practice for all believers. When there are
particular decisions to make or problems to face, it is important
to pray together as well as discuss together. It is also important
to learn how to apply the Bible to everyday decisions. Always
try to read the Bible with application in mind.

Christians need to belong to a church. In New Testament
days this was easy. Each new convert automatically belonged to
the church in the town where they lived. Each city or town had
only one church so there was no problem about which one to
belong to. Doubtless, some Christians lived at a distance from
any church, and of course this still happens today. Even if the
nearest church is some distance away and cannot be visited with
any regularity it is right to do so as often as is possible. In these
circumstances, it is also likely that the minister or some other
member (or members) of the church would visit such believers.

In normal circumstances it is important for husband and
wife to worship together regularly with the church—if there
are two services on the Lord's Day then be at both. Also, attend
any weeknight meetings for members. Churches are always
looking for those who can help with their different ministries.
However, especially once children have been born there needs
to be a balance between church and home. Husbands need to
help and relieve their wives once their own work is over. They
should not be so involved at church that they neglect either
wife or children.

Christians should have a right attitude towards money and
the things that money can buy. Paul says, 'Now there is great
gain in godliness with contentment, for we brought nothing into
this world, and we cannot take anything out of the world. But if

we have food and clothing, with these we will be content. But those who desire to be rich fall into temptation, into a snare, into many senseless and harmful desires that plunge people into ruin and destruction' (1 Timothy 6:6–9). To those who do have riches he says, 'As for the rich in this present age, charge them not to be haughty, nor to set their hopes on the uncertainty of riches, but on God, who richly provides us with everything to enjoy. They are to do good, to be rich in good works, to be generous and ready to share, thus storing up treasure for themselves as a good foundation for the future, so that they may take hold of that which is truly life' (1 Timothy 6:17–19).

Christians should not lead an extravagant lifestyle, or feel they have got to have every new thing that comes on the market. They are stewards of the money God has given them, and must use it wisely. In the Old Testament, God's people were to give a tenth of their income to the work of the Lord for the support of priests and Levites, widows, orphans and immigrants. Many Christians, and others, are very poor and need the help of those who have more. It is good for Christians to be given to hospitality and to use their home for relatives and friends, fellow believers and neighbours.

While the needs of the church for those who can help with its various ministries are important, Christians should also remember their local communities. There are often opportunities for believers to serve; perhaps on local councils, or in helping the socially disadvantaged. This may be an effective witness, even though it is not done directly through the church. However, a Christian couple will need to pray and think carefully so that they use their time and abilities in the best and most productive ways that they can. They will not be able to do everything they might wish to. They must choose wisely, balancing needs within the home with opportunities for service beyond it.

## 22. Bringing up children

Most marriages are between people who are young enough to have children and it will be the hope of the great majority that they will be able to start a family. This will not prove possible in every case. There are those whose union will never be fruitful because of some physical condition on the part of either husband or wife. So if, after a reasonable time, no children are conceived, medical investigation and help may be sought. Sometimes there are simple reasons for lack of conception which can be resolved. At other times, a couple has to accept the fact that no children will be born. This can be very hard to bear and both husband and wife need to avoid blaming the other. Rather, they should do their utmost to give mutual support and comfort.

The Bible speaks of a number of women who were barren, and shows the sorrow this can bring (cf. Genesis 30:1–2). Some who did eventually conceive had to wait for many years and then it took a miracle for conception to take place. Hard though it can be to accept that childlessness may prove to be the will of God, there are ways in which the pain can be eased. In some cases, adoption will be a possibility, and/or fostering, that is looking after children in need for short-term periods. There is a great deal of Christian work which can be done with children. Some who have never had their own children have been able to serve the Lord very effectively in this way.

Those who do have children need to be very understanding and sympathetic towards those who cannot conceive. In particular, some childless wives may feel they have failed as women. Not only married women, but single ones too can feel much the same sense of loss. It often needs real grace and thoughtfulness to avoid misunderstanding and a hurtful attitude. Proverbs 14:10 says, 'The heart knows its own bitterness.' Other people can sometimes be strangely blind to the sorrows that some experience.

When children are born this brings great joy. It also brings a new sense of responsibility and disrupts the normal pattern of life that the couple have established. Babies have to be fed during the night. The mother can get very tired and some may pass through a period of depression. This is a time for the husband to come to the rescue, insofar as he can. He will still have his work to do, but when he is at home he must play as much of a part as he can in helping his wife and relieving her. It is part of his responsibility to the God who gave him his wife and blessed them with a baby. He may need to learn quite a lot in a short time, but he can if he puts his mind to it!

All babies bring extra work, but some are born with disabilities of one sort or another. Some sleep quietly for long periods, others cry a lot and are very demanding. Even in difficult circumstances, try never to lose the sense of wonder at what seems the almost miraculous fruit of marital love. Babies are to be loved and cherished; they are gifts from God. It is a remarkable thing to be entrusted by him with a little child, and brings a great sense of responsibility. He who gave the gift also gives the grace to care for the little one.

Of course, grandparents are usually only too keen to help out in the early days. There may be other relatives too, including older children as time passes, who are able to help. A new baby is a gift for the wider family. Do not let anyone feel left out, who ought to feel included. Parents have the primary responsibility for bringing up their children, but they must avoid being over-protective. Other relatives, the church family and friends can all help, usually in unstructured ways through normal contact.

As children begin to grow in a Christian family, they should come to realise that their parents' Christian faith is an essential part of their life. Prayer to a heavenly Father, reading the Bible and attending the public worship of God are not things that are added on but are integral to the life of their parents. They need to learn that in times of illness, or when some decision needs to be taken or problem is faced, it is natural to turn to God for help and guidance. Children will gradually begin to sense if their parents' Christianity comes out of their hearts, or if it is just a traditional way of life they have fallen into.

From the very beginning, it is good for parents to pray over their children and then with them. If this is possible (and it isn't always) reading a short passage of Scripture and prayer at the beginning of the day—perhaps at the end of breakfast—starts the day well. In the early years, family prayers together, perhaps with the singing of a Christian hymn, should find a place somewhere in each day. The parent who puts a child to bed will pray before a goodnight kiss. As time goes by, children themselves often want to pray, and they should be given the opportunity to, both at night and in family prayers. A parent may need to give some guidance about praying, doing it wisely and helpfully.

As children get into their teens, parents may need to assess whether it is wise to continue with family prayers. Some teens resent feeling compelled to join in, and in those circumstances it would be better to discontinue such prayers together. If there are several children and they disagree among themselves about this, wisdom will be needed and can be sought from the Lord. In cases like this there is no set pattern that has to be followed. Indeed, it needs to be understood that all that is said here is not commanded in the Bible. This is guidance that fits in with biblical principles but has to be adapted to the circumstances of each family.

From an early age, children need to be guided and disciplined. This is positive to start with; they are to be shown what to do and how to behave. But they will not need to be shown how to be naughty and when they are, they need to be corrected. Parents correct their children because this is part of their responsibility, but also because they love their children and want the best for them. The Bible endorses this: 'Train up a child in the way he should go; even when he is old he will not depart from it' (Proverbs 22:6). Proverbs has a great deal to say about this. The same chapter speaks about 'the rod of discipline' (v.15; cf. v.8). It is not necessary to understand the word 'rod' to mean a literal stick; the word is often used simply to mean an instrument of correction—which may not be physical. Isaiah 11:4 speaks of 'the rod of his mouth' and in 1 Corinthians 4:21 Paul says to the Corinthians, 'Shall I come to you with a rod, or with love in a spirit of gentleness?'

In some countries, smacking is now forbidden by law and the law should be obeyed. In other parts of the world, it may be appropriate on occasions to smack a child with the hand (so that it hurts you too and you can feel that you are not smacking too hard). This should only take place when children are still fairly small. It is better for it to be done by mother rather than father, and this is essential in the case of girls. It is not helpful for children to grow up with the idea that mother is the loving parent, while father is the one who disciplines. As children grow older, suitable, different punishments should be used. Chastisement is to be done in love and for the child's good: 'For the Lord disciplines the one he loves, and chastises every son whom he receives … For what son is there whom his father does not discipline?' (Hebrews 12:6,7. The whole passage should be read).

However, before any such discipline, comes guidance and teaching. Remember, too, that we teach by our example as well as by what we say. Ephesians 6:4 says, 'Fathers, do not provoke your children to anger, but bring them up in the discipline and instruction of the Lord'. Children will be provoked if they are punished before they have been shown that what they are doing is wrong. They will be provoked if the punishment is excessive, or if it is just an angry reaction to the parent being disturbed. It is important, though, for children to know that 'No', means 'No'. Don't prohibit something before you consider whether it is wise to do so or not. When you do prohibit something then disobedience must be punished in an appropriate and proportionate way. In all normal circumstances, promises and warnings should always be carried out; your word is to be your word.

Parents naturally want to teach their children. From a fairly young age, children ask all sorts of questions and sometimes parents are hard put to give an answer. If it is a question that can be answered though you yourself don't know it, look it up in a book or on the internet. Take a real interest in your children's development. Point out interesting things when you go for a walk.

Help them understand the beauties of nature, but also buildings
and other objects made by people. Children learn best at their
own pace; don't force them, but don't leave them dissatisfied.
It is always better for them to learn from their parents rather
than from TV or the internet. If they need to be left to watch
TV, it is better to use videos you have already vetted, rather than
whatever programmes may be on. Many children's programmes
are not helpful for young children, and Christian parents will
need to be vigilant. Provide good things, so that you don't have
to say 'No' to harmful things.

All too quickly, they reach the age when they can go to school.
Some Christians parents prefer to home school their children.
This makes great demands, usually on the mother. It can be
done successfully and there are helpful materials that can be
bought and used. It is important, though, for your children
to have frequent contact with other children, so that they can
learn how to relate to their peers. In some countries there are
Christian schools, and provided the schools are able to reach
good standards, this may be best for children. Most children,
however, are likely to go to the local school.

How important it is for parents to encourage and help
their children while they are at school—but not by doing
their homework for them! It may be necessary to explain that
Christians have different beliefs and standards to those that
are taught at school. Do not undermine teachers. Explain that
there are many different ideas in the world and help your child
to understand why Christians believe what they do. It is right to
attend parents' evenings and to maintain as good a relationship
with the school and the children's teachers as possible. Children
from Christian homes are sometimes bullied. If this is serious
or persistent make sure you see the school authorities.

Teenage years can often be difficult. Teenagers are going through a period of change and adjustment. They know that they are growing up and yet sometimes they feel very vulnerable. Do not fuss over them, but be ready to support them. Do not try to interfere or run their lives for them, they will resent this and may turn against parents who do so. If they stay out very late or begin taking drugs or watching pornography or anything similar then you will need wisdom and firmness. Some may become quite antagonistic and rebellious; they may turn away from the Christian faith. Make sure they know you love them and will always help them, but give them space to find things out for themselves. Pray much for them in your private prayers.

# 23. Stresses and strains

Marriage is very seldom a smooth and easy journey through life together. Both husband and wife will find out things they did not know about the other. They will discover that they do not always think alike and that their tastes are not exactly the same. There will be times when they disagree, sometimes over important matters. There is nothing wrong with disagreements; it is how they are handled that is important. While, in general, a wife may defer to her husband, in matters which are more her concern, he should defer to her. When really important decisions have to be made it is much better if they can be talked through without either husband or wife having jumped to conclusions about what the outcome should be. Try to make sure that everything has been considered before a decision is attempted. Never start off simply with the intention of talking the other round. Consider all the facts and possibilities.

One possible source of friction is finance. Husband and wife need to agree early on about money matters. There are certain things to decide: for example, whether to have one bank account or two. This may depend on whether the wife is going to continue working. The question may need to be reconsidered with the birth of children. Circumstances, and possibly temperament, are likely to determine what is done. If finance is going to be tight, then both need to plan together and spend with care. Some people are too easy-going, others are too niggardly. Understand each other and work together. Unless circumstances are very difficult, each should know that there is some money that they can spend according to their own needs or desire.

Marriage brings together more than husband and wife; both will have their own parents, relatives and friends. It is not always easy to adapt and feel part of a family that you are not familiar with. There may well be some among family and friends who are not Christians. Usually an engaged couple will have already met with the other's parents, and perhaps any brothers or sisters. But it is one thing to come from the outside and meet the family, and quite another to feel that you belong. Consequently, it can take time to become really familiar with, and feel accepted by, in-laws. Unfortunately, sometimes there may be a measure of hostility from them. This makes for an awkward situation and Christians must do all they can to show forbearance and understanding, and try to make the relationship a happy one. Tension with in-laws can often also affect the relationship between husband and wife. Both sides should do all they can to prevent this happening.

We have different temperaments; some people are very placid, others can be easily roused. We should try to understand ourselves and our own weaknesses and guard against them. It is a very sad thing when husband and wife argue and lose their tempers with each other. We need to learn to guard our speech. There are two words that should not be used: 'never' and 'always'—as in 'You *never* do this' or 'You *always* say that'. When there has been a sharp disagreement, it is important to make up again afterwards. The one who starts off an argument is the one who should also apologise and take the lead in trying to put the relationship back on the right footing. The Bible has a lot to say about forgiveness and reconciliation. Christian people should be the best in exemplifying these qualities.

Allowances often have to be made. When children are small, mothers can lose a great deal of sleep and this inevitably affects them. When children are ill, this also can put a great strain on the parents, as can serious naughtiness. No-one knows when particular pressures are going to be put on them, but parents have to realise that this will happen from time to time. Exuberant children can sometimes be a trial to neighbours. Christian parents are naturally concerned if their children's behaviour is a source of grievance to the neighbours. They feel that their Christian witness is compromised. There is no easy solution to these things; sometimes neighbours are themselves pernickety and awkward. Simply be aware of matters like this. Pray for grace and wisdom and exercise a sensible discipline of children.

Illness is the common lot of fallen human beings. Some people are seldom ill, and then only with minor ailments. Others are prone to more serious sickness, either of body or mind. These facts are usually referred to in wedding services. Promises are made to love and honour 'in sickness and in health'. The couple take each other 'for better for worse, for richer for poorer, in sickness and in health'. Illness, especially chronic illness, puts demands on the marriage relationship. However, part of the blessing of marriage is that in a time of illness or weakness there is another who loves and who will care. Husbands generally find this more difficult than wives, but they must be prepared to learn.

Another source of possible friction can arise from employment.

Some jobs have fixed hours and may not be too stressful; other jobs can take a spouse away from home, sometimes for extended periods. Working with people, teaching children, nursing and social work can be very demanding and exhausting. These are occupations of importance in the community, which Christians often want to be involved in. Couples must be sensible about employment. If both want to work and both want to reach the top of their professions, it is likely that their relationship will suffer—probably greatly. Once two people are married, life is no longer about them as individuals. They are one together and must accept that purely individual ambitions have to be subjected to what is good for them together and their family.

This advice is presuming a marriage between two Christians. However, Christians can be at different stages in their spiritual lives. They can be subject to fierce temptations. They can lose a sense of assurance. They can sometimes wonder if they have been truly converted. They can lose their love for the Lord and backslide. They can change their views about church, or worship, or different aspects of Christian teaching. These things will inevitably test the relationship between husband and wife. They can lead to disagreements and tensions. One may need to help the other, or may have to bear with the other. If they have continued reading Scripture and praying together, this will be a great help. They may sometimes need help from a wise pastor and should be willing to accept it. Face these realities honestly and be humble and ready to learn and help each other. The greatest concern must be to please and honour God together.

# 24. Growing older

Not much will be said about this, important though it is, as this book is primarily directed to those considering marriage or recently married. However, marriage is for life, 'until death parts us', and this needs to be appreciated at the outset. So, in most cases the time will come when children have left home, when grandchildren may come to visit with their parents. Retirement takes place and the pace of life changes considerably. If the marriage has been strong throughout the ups and downs of many years, it is likely that it will remain like that. If both partners have been very busy in employment or in other ways, as they find their powers diminishing they will spend more time with each other. There may be more illness; frailty and weakness will gradually replace strength and ability.

This will test the depth of their love for one another as they come to rely more and more on each other. It is, though, a great thing to grow old for the glory of God; for the graces of patience, understanding, thoughtfulness and care to be manifested, often first by one partner, then by the other. There may sometimes be a sad period when there is much frailty in body or mind on the part of one or both.

Finally, the realisation that the relationship ends with the passing to glory of one partner lessens the sorrow for the one who remains, for it is certain that to be with Christ is far better (Philippians 1:23). If the couple all through their married life have trusted in the providential care and guidance of their Lord, then they know that whatever the latter days have for them, everything is under the gracious, sovereign control of the One who has watched over them through all their days. 'For this is God, our God forever and ever; he will be our guide even to death' (Psalm 48:14, NKJV).